DATE

Poetics of the New

The L=A=N=G=U=A=G=E Book
Edited by Bruce Andrews and Charles Bernstein

Dick Higgins, 1938–

HORIZONS
The Poetics and Theory of the Intermedia

Southern Illinois University Press
Carbondale and Edwardsville

Printed in the United States of America
Designed by Quentin Fiore
Production supervised by John DeBacher

Credits and acknowledgments: "Horizons" appears also
in Stephen Foster, ed., *Perspectives on the Avant Garde*
(Iowa City: University of Iowa Press, 1983) and as
"Horizonte" in *Sprache im technischen ZeiTalter* 85
(January-March 1983): 33–47. "Intermedia" first
appeared in *Something Else Newsletter,* vol. 1, no. 1 (©
1966 by Something Else Press, Inc.). "The Strategy of
Visual Poetry: Three Aspects" appeared in *Precisely,*
nos. 3–5 (1979). "Points Towards a Taxonomy of Sound
Poetry" appeared in *Precisely,* no. 10/11/12 (1981).
"Underpiece/Overpiece" is copyright © 1979 by Richard
C. Higgins. "Postmodern Performance: Some Criteria
and Common Points" first appeared in A. A. Bronson
and Peggy Gale, eds., *Performance by Artists* (Toronto:
Art Metropole, 1979). "A Child's History of Fluxus" first
appeared in *Lightworks,* no. 11/12 (Fall, 1979). All the
above are copyright © by their publishers in the years
indicated.

Library of Congress Cataloging in Publication Data
Higgins, Dick, 1938–
   Horizons, the poetics and theory of the intermedia.

   (Poetics of the new)
   Includes index.
    1. Avant-garde (Aesthetics)—History—20th century.
2. Arts, Modern—20th century. I. Title. II. Series.
NX458.H5 1983   700'.9'04   83-4720
ISBN 0-8093-1142-9

Contents

1 Horizons

"I am devoted to the idea of burying the avant-garde."—Rosalind Kraus, critic, at a conference at the University of Iowa in April 1981

Preamble The history of most arts is the history of their avant-gardes, of those works and groupings of works which the next generation seizes upon to follow, thus provoking the analogy to the avant-garde of an army (the small group of soldiers which precedes the main body of troups); but those works which are truly avant-garde are by their very nature apt to be a little strange to most viewers at the time of their origin, even to seem unpopular or elitist because they simply do not fit the establishment's norms. Why are avant-garde works of such critical importance historically? There are two basic reasons: (1) by definition, avant-garde work minimalizes traditional models, and therefore there tends to be an active, dialectical interrelationship between the form which a work assumes and the *material* of which it consists. The *material* is not channeled into an existing mode, but, rather, uses whatever uniqueness there is in the material to determine itself. (2) This channeling process, minimizing previous models, uses the experience and moment of existence of its maker, the artist, and therefore reflects the newly unique thing about its moment in history—the up-to-now-this-wouldn't-have-been-possible.

I am not speaking here of the "pop-garde" with its upper-class Bohemian overtones. Just at this moment (1981) in visual art, for instance, that would include Jasper Johns, James Rosenguist, Saul LeWitt, or Judy Chicago. They belong to the follow-the-leader world of charm, fashionable but safe dissent, and high style. However, such work tends to lack implications for further innovations and for holistic mental experiences. It lives off the real world, taking from it more than it contributes to it in terms of deep meaningfulness, mentally or spiritually or emotionally.

And, of course, beyond the "avant-pop" there is

the deliberately deeply conservative art which most people think of when we say "art"—this would include most figurative art of this moment (including most, but not all, political art) and most geometrical art (although that too has its "pop-garde:" Sol LeWitt and Lawrence Poons, for example). The conservative artists tend to use forms which are remembered; these are brought to bear on the *material* in remembered ways rather than in ways determined by the *material*. Thus they often have more to do with memory of art than with the objective World outside their makers, and with the traditions grouping such memories —classic, romantic, "formal," "socialist realistic" and so on. Of course as any avant-garde becomes old, its constituent parts will tend to join this newly conservative area; but this process and its phenomenology are not my concern at this time.

One of the things that a bad critic or theorist tends to do is to make sher viewpoint (his or hers) into a Procrustean bed, into which any work at hand or theoretical *material* is compelled to fit, regardless of the consequences, either by stretching it beyond recognizability or by lopping off parts of it by ignoring them; such a critic presents only sher own horizon of experience and ignores that of the reader or listener, who may have sher own perspective on the work or on the *material*. On the other hand, the good critic tends to point out the implications of the *material* and work, developing any theory not a priori but from a dialectical relationship with the *material* and by contextualizing it. Such a critic should be attracted to the avant-garde as a matter of course, because the avant-garde can be viewed at firsthand and free of codifications into what may become its eventual subsumptions of traditions and modes; thus the avant-garde, once identified, is at least for a time not subject to the misinformation that leads to criticism *from* the false theory or horizon I have described. Furthermore, in the avant-garde one sees the artist dealing with sher moment and its needs, and thus the critic can, by focusing on these, contextualize works which reflect them into their moments of origin. Such a critic can place, to choose extreme examples, both Horace and Monteverdi and

Cézanne into their own decades and moments of history, and can also, by doing this, fix them in their relevance to the critic's own decade in terms of their *Zeitgeist* and achievements and his or hers, thus establishing what I have called elsewhere a "dialectic of centuries,"[1] describing the work according to its own perceived moments in time, class, culture, and so on, as related to the critic's or theorist's own moment in time, class, culture, and so on. The pleasure of reading great criticism is that the reader compares sher own horizon with the critic's and thus develops sher own insights, even when the reader disagrees with those of the critic. In such criticism we get a dialectic not just of time but of class and culture as well. At such a point we can say that great criticism—Hazlitt's, for example—becomes art, the art of literature. No horizon overwhelms the others, and thus a fusion of these horizons (*Horizontverschmelzung* is Hans-Georg Gadamer's term) becomes the objective. It is the exploration of the processes surrounding horizons which is my concern here, and it is to that to which we will now proceed. However we must note first that for such a fusion of horizons to occur, the reader or listener must have some consciousness of sher own horizons in order to have something to blend with those of the critic. We should also note that a great deal of the criticism—so-called theory— which is in vogue just now, especially that favored by the Mafia of the Rue Jacob (structuralism, poststructuralism, post-poststructuralism, and so on, all of which are Variations on a Theme by Saussure with pretentions toward objective truth which are hard to accept), a great deal of such criticism really is not valuable inasmuch as it presents no dialectic with its *material* and allows no process of fusion of the horizons of the reader and the critic. Perhaps it is needed by our academic mills for some heuristic purpose or other, but it has no significance to people whose object is to live a deep cultural life and to do so by experiencing art as part of their ongoing existance.

---

[1]Dick Higgins, *A Dialectic of Centuries: Notes Towards a Theory of the New Arts,* 2d ed. (New York: Printed Editions, 1979), hereafter called *Dialectic,* see pp. 156–66.

Art as Paradigm　One frequently found variety of avant-garde art today is what I have called "exemplative."[2] This is art in which the work is not a definitive realization of some kind but is, rather, an example—one possibility, or a sampling of possible realizations.[3] By implying its set of alternatives, the viewer, faced with such a work and seeing these in sher imagination, projects sher own horizon and fuses it with that of the artist. The artist's paradigmatic realization is compared by the viewer with sher own.

Nor need such work necessarily be only of the cooler, relatively cerebral kind. There can also be what I have called an "allusive referential" at work,[4] a displacement between what one expects to see or what one would logically regard as normative and what one does, in fact, see (or hear or read). This displacement factor can generate the entire emotional panoply of which art is capable without any particular reference to the artist's or viewer's personal expression. We expect to see or hear A, instead of which we see or hear B, and this points toward a new entity, C. This can only occur when there is an interaction between our own horizons and that of the artist's, which we then experience as a process of entering the artist's world and feeling ourselves doing so. This allusive referential process is not, of course, unique to exemplative art or even to avant-garde art. We experience it intuitively when we hear the opening passage of Beethoven's Fifth Symphony and suddenly sense that the rhythm refers back to an opening silence, beginning with a rest— resulting in a heightened sense of drama on the part of the perceptive listener. Furthermore, we experience it when we listen to Anton von Webern's Symphony and we try to second-guess the composer as to the next note we will hear; constantly and consistently we are confronted by a displacement process as profound as that in a Bach fugue, and to the extent of our willingness to be involved in von Webern's process we

---

[2]"An Exemplativist Manifesto," in *Dialectic,* see pp. 156–66.

[3]*Dialectic,* pp. 23–27, 158–166.

[4]*Dialectic,* pp. 67–74.

experience a strange sense of space activated by emotion.

But it is in exemplative art—musical realizations of works by Cage, sound poems and aleotoric works by myself or Jackson Mac Low or many of the current European avant-garde, that this allusive referential is useful to explain why the work does not simply leave even a sophisticated listener "cold" as it were, but continues to engage him or her.

We can also see here why it is valuable to the "receiver," as we might call the listener, viewer, or reader collectively, not to be too preoccupied with sher own identity or private, personal consciousness in any unique or linear sense. If the receiver allows sher own horizon to overwhelm that of the artist—or, worse yet, if the receiver totally concentrates on attempting to read such a consciousness into the paradigmatic sampled work at hand, the reader will fail to achieve the fusion of horizons and will thus miss the opportunity to enjoy the work. Such a receiver is involved in a self-cognitive process which does not belong in the fusion process as one finds it in exemplative art. In fact it seems to be very characteristic of our arts since the mid-1950s that such self-cognition is counterproductive to the art experience, both for the receiver and also for the artist. Thus, and for this reason, I have suggested a way of regarding the break of the period since the mid-1950s with its previous period, not according to the recently traditional subsumption of *modern/postmodern,* with a number of movements and subcategories in that flow, but rather as *cognitive/postcognitive* using "cognitive" with the caveat that it is such with regard to the sense of self or personal identity on the part of the artist or receiver.[5] The two approaches are not, of course, contradictory by any means. But the usefulness of using the *cognitive/postcognitive* distinction is that

1. it allows for a projection back into like works from the past for which there is a similar postcognitive sense without elaborate historical

[5]*Dialectic,* pp. 7–9, 93–101, 158–60, 163–66.

justifications—e.g., works by Gertrude Stein, Erik Satie, Marcel Duchamp, James Joyce, and so on, can be put in a neater lineage with the present avant-garde than the modern/postmodern dichotomy allows.

2. It allows us to deal with the commonality of such artists as I have just listed and those of today without worrying about precisely to what art movement or tendency such-and-such artist belongs. It decentralizes movements in general, reducing them to statistical quantifications of how much the artist does this or that, rather than requiring that the technical practice of the artist be justified by some artificial ideology. Movements, if one accepts the cognitive/postcognitive distinction, become a matter for the journalists and public-relations-minded curators and academics, not something that serious people need attach any great significance. Just to focus on recent years, all the recent so-called movements—abstract expressionism, neo-dada, pop art, concrete poetry, fluxus, sound poetry, minimal art, postminimal art, happenings, which are no more movements than, for example, "collage" was a movement [surely if collage began today some bright critic or art history professor would create the ideology of "collagism"!],—can be seen as technical trends or tendencies, each with works contained within it that justify it as a formal approach. By using my suggested distinction, cognitive/postcognitive, we can concentrate instead on classes of psychological models for artist, artwork, and receiver.

The Erotic of Fusion   The desire to fuse seems to be a part of our biological nature as living beings. Paramecia "conjugate"—i.e., they fuse, and some of the substance of one passes into the substance of another. People fuse, not just in the act of love, but also in the state of being in love. Perhaps it can even be argued that to some extent they fuse in friendship, with its give and take and deep involvements. But certainly there is an erotic element inherent in the approach to art as the "fusing of horizons." Naturally such a fusion is less likely to be permanent than it is to be temporary or "marginal" or "liminal" (from *limen,* the Latin word for "threshold"), this last a term popularized by the anthropologist, Victor Turner. One enters onto a threshold experience which, following Turner's practice, I will call liminal, and one views the world within. One visits the abode of the Gods, or perhaps of Beauty or Love or Form. Or the view is into the world of the nightmare, which warns and possibly purges us. But we do not plan to stay there. We cannot experience, with all our attention, music or theater or philosophical principles or sex or even religion twenty-four hours a day. But we do return from the liminal experience enriched. We return to the everyday world, and the experience becomes marginal with regard to our daily, normative existence; but the liminal experience has refreshed us and can be a source of energy and meaning for us. In our spiritual lives we often, even, praise the lack of desire to hang onto the liminal experience; we commend the attitude of "letting go" afterward. The Buddha comes out from under the bo tree and shares his enlightenment. We attend a gathering in the green room after an extraordinary performance, and we see the performer who, a few moments before, seemed nearly out of control—bad, bizarre, transfigured into a being from another world. The performer is smoking a cigarette, chatting with friends and well-wishers, in some degree of dishabille. Far from this transformation detracting from our perceptions of what we have seen, we tend to admire the performer all the more for sher control. The world of the spirits (or the spiritual or the beautiful or the exaggeratedly satyrical or the nightmarish) has been visited, and now it is left behind. Our shamanistic ancestors visited such worlds to bring back magic into daily lives; we lack their belief in such magic, but nonetheless we experience something of it through our artistic lives. The earliest Christians sought miracles in their saints' lives; the modern Christians find their miraculous in the dailiness of existence, and the intense experience of the liminal comes, instead, from the rituals of their faith. The art experience carries with it something of the liminality of religion, especially for those to whom religion has become a closed book or a threat. And to those who follow the avant-garde, the very newness of the new art carries with it some of this liminality; it seems to suggest hope and meaning. One looks to the new for a better future for the arts, for some measure of renewal for ourselves. When our horizons seem tired, we fuse them with the horizons of the new artists, and we hope, at least, that, some of the time, we will experience renewal through this fusion in a way which we cannot get from fusing our horizons with those of artists of the past. Not that this last is in any way less valid, of course—the fusion of our horizons with those of a Goethe, a Mahler, a Li Po, or a Hokusai or Michelangelo, such fusions are equally profound and renew our sense of our roots. They point to the possibility of greatness in our species in a way that is unlikely with the numerical majority of our avant-garde in our own time. But it is in this avant-garde that we see our own world mirrored and not the worlds of the past or of some other space or culture. Ours is the only time that any of us will ever know at firsthand, uninterpreted through the eyes of historians. So it is in our own avant-garde to which we turn, hoping always for the liminal and transforming miracle. Unfortunately we seldom find it. But once in a great while we *do* experience it. Through the fusion process we hear, with a shock, our own voice speaking to us, our own age. The liminal magic occurs, and we are renewed, uniquely so.

And ever thereafter we hunger for this magic to recur. Our sense of our own horizons is deepened, and we look on and on through the avant-garde for the liminal fusion. The great works of the past no longer provide us with the experience we are seeking, however wonderful they are. For this, it is not among the perfect voices of the past that we must look but, rather, among the mostly unsatisfactory voices of our present, knowing that these are at least alive. One is not searching out the memory of the perfect lover but, rather, for the warm and living lover.

Thus this fusion is a basic hunger in us. Without it as an ideal we feel incomplete, like the lovers in Plato's *Phaedrus* who need their other halves to feel complete. We fuse in pleasure as in mind or soul. We fuse our present horizons with our past ones; isn't that what biography and autobiography are really about? We desire, not in the mechanical sense of inexhaustible cravings, to possess (against which, for example, most religions warn us—one need only think, for instance, of the Buddhists' "Four Vows" on this point: "Desires are inexhaustible; I vow to put an end to them"), but rather we desire for its own sake, because the liminal fusion has, at one time, happened to us and the desire has become a part of our cultural being. The desire is part of the ongoing process of the fusion—its projection onto us and into the future, and through it we come to know ourselves culturally with ever-expanding circles of information and experience. Thus, any art which offers such fusion with new horizons is the only one which can be relied on to offer a new intermesh of our horizons with new ones, and at best our experience of them will always have, be it ever so tragical or disturbing, some element of pleasure, which can be called an erotic.

But thinking along the lines of such nonpersonal fusion we might well come to a sort of hebephrenia, which is the medical term for the pathological state in which one attempts to avoid all personal expression. In fact, for example, that is one of the things that the new arts are often accused of. For example, Theodore Adorno attributed hebephrenia to Stravinsky in his book *On Modern Music* back in the 1930s. What ever would he say, then, about the new postcognitive arts, such as those of John Cage, Marcel Duchamp, Robert Smithson, Robert Morris, or Dieter Roth, in which, even more, any personal expression would be an unwarranted intrusion on the part of the artist? But in the new arts, such an intrusion would reduce the horizon by overparticularizing it. The horizon would become opaque and would reveal only the face of the artist, thus preventing the viewer from seeing through it to sher own horizon in order to fuse with it. To a näive critic, the new arts seem cold or cerebral, since such a critic does not know where to look for the experience which is at its heart. The technique of fusion has not yet been learned by many people—and all erotics *must* be learned, which can be a difficult and even, sometimes, painful or awkward process.

However we can distinguish between the use of expression in the *material* of art work, and the use of expression to reveal the subjective persona of the artist. This last would be the way of the cognitive artist, while the former has its place in the work of the non- or postcognitive artist. In fact very few expressive materials are beyond the pale in the new arts. For example, since screaming is one of the hallmarks of expressionist art in the early part of this century—one can think of the various versions of the Edvard Munch woodcuts and paintings of "The Scream" or of the theater of Antonin Artaud—one might imagine that a scream would be very hard for a new artist to use. But in my fluxus piece, "Danger Music No. 17" (1962) I invite the performer to scream as loud as possible, with no context offered, until the performer is physically near collapse. Traditionally I have done this in the dark, so that each receiver is separated by the darkness from each other receiver and from sher perception of my physical presence (or that of any other performer). What one receives in such an experience is not a personal, specific screamed expression but, rather, an *example* of a scream, so that one directly experiences screams in general and the receiver must deal with sher own experience of screams. Thus, however expressive the language of this piece, the receiver's attention is not directed toward the individuality or persona of myself or of any other performer but toward the horizon of the screamed event and toward sher own experience or horizon of screams. These fuse, hopefully, and, also hopefully, the liminal experience occurs on the emotional level as well as the intellectual one. In the expressionistic model of the artist, where the art exists in order to express the composer or writer or whatever, there is always the danger that the fusion will fail, that the receiver will find the expressionistic artist silly, that the work will seem, in Gertrude Stein's phrase, "more excit*ed* than excit*ing*." In the postcognitive, exemplative model, to which my "Danger Music No. 17" belongs, the receiver is invited to forget the screamer in favor of the scream. The actor becomes an *en*actor. The horizons, if the performance works, fuse. And in no good performance of the many that I have seen has anyone ever laughed.

Thus, with sher eye of shemself and onto sher horizon, the exemplative artist finds shemself less involved in the conception of a work than in the perception of it. One examines the *material* and does what it seems to suggest. Thus the centrality of found materials in the new arts, from Duchamp's *objets trouvés* or the found materials of the dadaists, through to such related modes of using found materials as, in recent American literature, the writings of Charles Olson or Paul Metcalf, although both of these tend toward noncognitivism without ever quite getting there. Thus the centrality too of photography in the new arts, since photography always has a found element, and making a photograph is at least as much a matter of perceiving it in the *material* as of taking it from its old context and, by means of an aparatus, producing a picture from it. One enters into a dialectical relationship with the materials at hand, what I have been calling the *material*. An example would be photographs by Ralph Meatyard, Clarence John Laughlin or by Minor White.

In general, then, the artist discovers what he or she is seeing, hearing, considering; the artist does what the *material* suggests, the receiver empathizes with it and experiences its principles both physically, intellectually and intuitively; one accepts the experience, one fuses the work with what one knows and the projected horizon with one's own, and the fusion fulfills the erotic in the process.

But Why Go through All This?   Currently in vogue is the structuralist/poststructuralist nexus of theory and cultural criticism. These treat culture as language and discuss it in terms of linguistics, creating a new sense of right and wrong by appeal to scientific validity; yet the approach lacks any real scientific method, since it is in no way inductive. Its practitioners defend their approach on the ground that what they are doing is the science of literary theory; yet they also lack the dialectical ratiocination which we expect from the best scientific papers as a matter of course, so that anything scientific in their work is science-as-metaphor rather than science-qua-science. Thus Claude Levi-Strauss treats anthropology according to linguistic modes and metaphors, producing structuralist anthropology. Thus Jacques Lacan, ever the poet, applies linguistics (mostly in the name of de Saussure) to the psyche, producing structuralist poetic psychology. Thus Roland Barthes, perhaps the subtlest of the structuralists, applies linguistics to criticism, producing the models of structuralist criticism, the most striking of which is perhaps the book *S/Z*, an incredibly detailed analysis of a short story by Balzac; it is, however, a work based on one single work of literature and that from one single epoch, the nineteenth century (as are all works, of course), and the problem with using this one work as a universal paradigm is that any relevance which it has is based on this one kind of work. Barthes's theory, then, is drawn from only one kind of work, and it is inadequate when it comes to the present avant-garde (or, indeed, to many other kinds of work, ancient or non-Western or baroque, for example). Alas, *S/Z* and Barthes's theory that is drawn from it as a universal finds its limits when we try to explain the startling effect of Stein's aphorism scientifically through linguistics. It simply is not appropriate. Semiotics can be defined as "the study of how things mean, and of what signals and conveys meaning," and it is a perfectly valid subject for literary and cultural inquiry, as it has been since the earliest work of semiotics with which I am familiar, Giordano Bruno's fascinating text from 1591, *De Imaginum, Signorum, et Idearum Compositione* (On the Composition of Images, Signs, and ideas).[6] The trouble with many recent works of semiotics is that it too is semiotics for its own sake, as if the subject of a work could guarantee its relevance. Yet book after book of semiotics has appeared, many of them published by the very influential Editions de

---

[6]Giordano Bruno, "De Imaginum, Signorum, et Idearum Compositione," in *Jordani Bruni Nolani Opere Latine Conscripta,* 3 vols. in 8 pts. (1889; Bad Cannstatt b. Stuttgart: Friedrich Frommann Verlag, 1962), vol. 3, pp. 8–318. Modern edition cited to indicate availability.

Seuil at 27 rue Jacob in Paris—hence my reference at the beginning of this essay to the Mafia of that address. One suspects that the recent emergence of "poststructuralism" (the work of Jacques Derrida and his followers, which seems to consist of structuralism enriched by Heidegger, Hegel, Genet, and with a hermetic use of language from pataphysics, for all that it purports to be a successor to structuralism), that the emergence of this "movement" is artificial, launched by the publisher's sales department when sales of structuralist books began to fall off. In any case, poststructuralism seems to serve the needs of academic fashions and the publishing industry more than that of the millions of would-be horizons-users around the world.

An anecdote: one of the most notable theorists in this vein is the Yale University French professor, Paul de Man. Once when he had given an incredibly involuted lecture on the development and nature of structuralism/poststructuralism, I asked him: *"What is the erotic of your work?"* Had I posed such a question to a Heidegger or even a Lyotard, either could have answered me; in fact, Lyotard once did, with great gusto. But Paul de Man could not. On the one hand it was clear that I was not looking simply for a part of his lecture which would provide a simple pleasure principle, as in Horace's formulation that "art should delight and instruct." But instead he tried to justify his lecture—his work—with an appeal to the truth: "it is valuable because it is true." I then asked him *"For what is it true?"* This he tried to answer with the usual arguments, in general, against pragmatism and for theoretical researches. But he was totally unable to deal with the inner logic of my question of the teleology of truth. Well, perhaps it *is* true that all art is capable of being treated as some sort of language—but it is only a metaphor that art is language, and the problem arises when one loses sight of this and proposes to treat a metaphorical truth as an absolute one.

Theory is at its best when it is not of this sort, but when it proposes to delineate and explore the underpinnings of its *material*. The *material* of cultural criticism can include horizons, for instance. But it is very hard for an academic critic to be a good theorist, because his eye is not on the nature and teleology of his argument, but rather on its teachability, defensibility, and salability. He or she asks not "what does this mean to me?" of an argument, but "can I teach it and defend it?" A great critic offers us diamonds for our consideration and, if they prove to be faulty, either cuts the diamonds over or tosses them away. An academic critic has sher job at stake and thus must defend sher diamond, be it ever so faulty, for the sake of sher job. The academic critic tends always to seek to add to the dignity of sher profession; thus the appeal of a formula of another Yale academic, Harold Bloom—and Yale *does* seem like a colony of the Rue Jacob—"the meaning of a poem is a poem." If a critic expounds a meaning and that meaning is a poem, why then the critic is suddenly a poet, and is probably a far more respectable one, one with far fewer rough edges, than a real-life nonacademic poet.

My point is not to attack academia as such but only to criticize its pretensions and limitations in order to explain why structuralism and poststructuralism are as they are, so that the other models I have proposed can be seen as possibly more useful. Indeed, the currently fashionable modes practical criticism—movement and descriptive criticism—are equally based on illusion. The journalist critics concentrate on whatever is most in fashion or at hand and ignore the rest, even when information concerning it is available to them. Such criticism tends, when viewed from the vantage point of an avant-garde, to seem like a gargantuan synechdoche— describing the whole of an art in terms of its most obvious parts. We ask someone to give us a hand, meaning they should help us not only with their hands but with their sense as well. But the journalists speak of the art of today only in terms of what the fashionable galleries promote. We would not think highly of a critic who called a man a "prick" or a woman a "cunt," but the journalist critics do just that to art when they harp on the details of the art world in the name of the whole thing. Few critics have the arrogance of the *New York Times*'s Hilton Kramer, who simply denies the existence of an avant-garde (though he sometimes speaks highly of individual avant-garde artists a decade or so after their work has moved into the larger, more predictable world of official art). Most simply invent "movements" to attach to their names—or, in the case of the literary critics, unnecessary categories. Most write about dull subjects—the works given to the world by the art gallery industry, the publishing industry, and so on (works which are easily packaged as commodity rather than works which, by their very nature, pose problems)—so that no matter how well they write, any intelligence they have is somehow wasted. If a critic uses for sher subject merely the materials which are most at hand or fashionable, then one's critiques belong, de facto if not de jure by intention, to the history of fashion more than to the world of valuable culture.

Such critics are wasting their lives (and our time). If a critic is to offer any sort of horizon to posterity, it must be from the perspective that "this is one of the most unique and characteristic works I have encountered, and here is why." To return to the point I made earlier, an idea which I first heard from the composer Earle Brown, the only art that we will ever know at firsthand is the art of our own time, and by extension, the avant-garde is the part of that art in which the next time originates. Thus for a critic to ignore the avant-garde is to guarantee sher own irrelevance. Even if one is writing about the arts of the past—Shakespeare or Goya, let's say—we must have a sense that the writing is taking place from what the critic knows, which is to say, from sher own time. We must have a sense that it comes from *a present,* otherwise the horizon is lost and the critique is so much academic masturbation, so much secondhand hearsay.

Emigré Arts: Other Horizons and Fusions Besides the postcognitive tendency in the new arts, another characteristic of many of them is that they are intermedial, that is, they fall conceptually between established or traditional media. Thus, concrete and other visual poetries fall conceptually between visual art and literature. Intermedia differ from mixed media; an opera is a mixed medium, inasmuch as we know what is the music, what is the text, and what is the mise-en-scéne. In an intermedium, on the other hand, there is a conceptual fusion. Concrete and some of the other visual poetries are intermedial; they lie *between* literature and visual art, and there is fusion between these so that we cannot deal with just one of their origins but must deal with the work as both visual and literary art. An art song has a text and music; it is a mixed medium. But sound poetry has music penetrating to the very core of the poem's being, or literature at the marrow of the heard experience; it is an intermedium. These are other fusions—the fusions within the artist's own horizons, sher sense of what is on the music horizon fused with what is on the literature horizon for example. We view the work, and our own horizons fuse accordingly; this can be satisfying—though we are usually also conscious of the tendency of such intermedia to become, with familiarity, simply new media.

Other kinds of fusion than media are also possible. Postminimal art and fluxus, for example, fuse philosophical principles or structures with their "serious culture" referents; the art/life dichotomy becomes the art-life fusion. Perhaps one could even argue that structuralist criticism at its best, in such works as the Barthes *S/Z,* is intermedial between art and sociology; but the structuralists seem unconscious of this possibility. And surely happenings are a three-way fusion between theater, music, and visual art; are perhaps art performances, so prevalent just now (1981), a five-way fusion, between theater, literature, music, visual art, and life? In any case, the intermedial nature of a work is certainly no guarantee of its quality or relevance, any more than the novelty element of an avant-garde work guarantees its ongoing interest. Stressing either of these too much would be putting the cart before the horse. The point is that many of the interesting works of the avant-garde are intermedial and allow for fusions on a nonpsychological plane, and that many of the interesting works of the avant-garde offer some degree of novelty because of the conditions of their existence. We should not reject the avant-garde work because it does not match our previous notions of art, but we should look to intermedial works for the new possibilities of fusion which they afford.

What does this mean? To me it means that the areas of our experience have taken on dialectical relationships of their own. Painting has ceased to be a matter of paint staying on the canvas in the world of visual art, but instead painting has come to migrate, abstracting itself from its traditional bases, entering the world outside of itself, interacting and fusing with other media to form visual poetry, visual music, these in turn to become new media capable of migrating yet further. Our sense of music is modified by the penetration from visual art. And so, too, with the other arts. Admittedly today we have only ten thousand in the audience for this process, but tomorrow it will be a hundred thousand and later a million more. That is at the very nature of the concept of an avant-garde—it precedes the mass of troops.

The study of these projections, migrations, and fusions will be the semiotics of the fusion of horizons, of the *Horizontverschmelzung,* the hermeneutics of which is an area of criticism which we desperately need, and of which we have thus far been deprived because of the academics' subservience to fashion. We need this methodology of interpretation, which is what I take hermeneutics to be, in order to help us all, as participants in our culture, to give us appropriate ways and understandings of our horizons and of the implied horizons of the works which we encounter. We cannot allow any one such migration over the others—applying linguistic approaches to our culture is only one of the many possibilities, and a monodiet is unwholesome for any living organism. Instead we need a pluralistic approach, recognizing that a horizon has many many points along it as the eye moves back and forth. If a horizon is bent, there may be multiple points of intersection and highly complex fusions. Until we have come to deal with this, our criticism remains inadequate.

2 Intermedia

1965 Much of the best work being produced today seems to fall between media. This is no accident. The concept of the separation between media arose in the Renaissance. The idea that a painting is made of paint on canvas or that a sculpture should not be painted seems characteristic of the kind of social thought—categorizing and dividing society into nobility with its various subdivisions, untitled gentry, artisans, serfs and landless workers—which we call the feudal conception of the Great Chain of Being. This essentially mechanistic approach continued to be relevant throughout the first two industrial revolutions, just concluded, and into the present era of automation, which constitutes, in fact, a third industrial revolution.

However, the social problems that characterize our time, as opposed to the political ones, no longer allow a compartmentalized approach. We are approaching the dawn of a classless society, to which separation into rigid categories is absolutely irrelevant. This shift does not relate more to East than West or vice versa. Castro works in the cane fields. New York's Mayor Lindsay walks to work during the subway strike. The millionaires eat their lunches at Horn and Hardart's. This sort of populism is a growing tendency rather than a shrinking one.

We sense this in viewing art which seems to belong unnecessarily rigidly to one or another form. We view paintings. What are they, after all? Expensive, handmade objects, intended to ornament the walls of the rich or, through their (or their government's) munificence, to be shared with large numbers of people and give them a sense of grandeur. But they do not allow of any sense of dialogue.

Pop art? How could it play a part in the art of the future? It is bland. It is pure. It uses elements of common life without comment, and so, by accepting the misery of this life and its aridity so mutely, it condones them. Pop and op are both dead, however, because they confine themselves, through the media which they employ, to the older functions of art, of decorating and suggesting grandeur, whatever their detailed content of their artists' intentions. None of the ingenious theories of the Mr. Ivan Geldoway combine can prevent them from being colossally boring and irrelevant. Milord runs his Mad Avenue Gallery, in which he displays his pretty wares. He is protected by a handful of rude footmen who seem to feel that this is the way Life will always be. At his beck and call is Sir Fretful Callous, a moderately well-informed high priest, who apparently despises the Flame he is supposed to tend and therefore prefers anything which titillates him. However, Milord needs his services, since he, poor thing, hasn't the time or the energy to contribute more than his name and perhaps his dollars; getting information and finding out what's going on are simply toooooo exhausting. So, well protected and advised, he goes blissfully through the streets in proper Louis XIV style.

This scene is not just characteristic of the painting world as an institution, however. It is absolutely natural to (and inevitable in) the concept of the pure medium, the painting or precious object of any kind. That is the way such objects are marketed since that is the world to which they belong and to which they relate. The sense of "I am the state," however, will shortly be replaced by "After me the deluge," and, in fact, if the High Art world were better informed, it would realize that the deluge has already begun.

Who knows when it began? There is no reason for us to go into history in any detail. Part of the reason that Duchamp's objects are fascinating while Picasso's voice is fading is that the Duchamp pieces are truly between media, between sculpture and something else, while a Picasso is readily classifiable as a painted ornament. Similarly, by invading the land between collage and photography, the German John Heartfield produced what are probably the greatest graphics of our century, surely the most powerful political art that has been done to date.

The ready-made or found object, in a sense an intermedium since it was not intended to conform to the pure medium, usually suggests this, and therefore suggests a location in the field between the general area of art media and those of life media. However, at this time, the locations of this sort are relatively unexplored, as compared with media between the arts. I cannot, for example, name work which has consciously been placed in the intermedium between painting and shoes. The closest thing would seem to be the sculpture of Claes Oldenburg, which falls between sculpture and hamburgers or Eskimo Pies, yet it is not the sources of these images themselves. An Oldenburg Eskimo Pie may look something like an Eskimo Pie, yet is neither edible nor cold. There is still a great deal to be done in this direction in the way of opening up aesthetically rewarding possibilities.

In the middle 1950s many painters began to realize the fundamental irrelevance of abstract expressionism, which was the dominant mode at the time. Such painters as Allan Kaprow and Robert Rauschenberg in the United States and Wolf Vostell in Germany turned to collage or, in the latter's case, dé-collage, in the sense of making work by adding or removing, replacing and substituting or altering components of a visual work. They began to include increasingly incongruous objects in their work. Rauschenburg called his constructions "combines" and went so far as to place a stuffed goat—spattered with paint and with a rubber tire around its neck—onto one. Kaprow, more philosophical and restless, meditated on the relationship of the spectator and the work. He put mirrors into his things so the spectator could feel included in them. That wasn't physical enough, so he made enveloping collages which surrounded the spectator. These he called "environments." Finally, in the spring of 1958, he began to include live people as part of the collage, and this he called a "happening."

The proscenium theater is the outgrowth of seventeenth-century ideals of social order. Yet there is remarkably little structural difference between the dramas of Davenant and those of

Edward Albee, certainly nothing comparable to the difference in pump construction or means of mass transportation. It would seem that the technological and social implications of the first two industrial revolutions have been evaded completely. The drama is still mechanistically divided: there are performers, production people, a separate audience and an explicit script. Once started, like Frankenstein's monster, the course of affairs is unalterable, perhaps damned by its inability to reflect its surroundings. With our populistic mentality today, it is difficult to attach importance—other than what we have been taught to attach—to this traditional theater. Nor do minor innovations do more than provide dinner conversation: this theater is round instead of square, in that one the stage revolves, here the play is relatively senseless and whimsical (Pinter is, after all, our modern J. M. Barrie—unless the honor belongs more properly to Beckett). Every year fewer attend the professional Broadway theaters. The shows get sillier and sillier, showing the producers' estimate of our mentality (or is it their own that is revealed?). Even the best of the traditional theater is no longer found on Broadway but at the Judson Memorial Church, some miles away. Yet our theater schools grind out thousands on thousands of performing and production personnel, for whom jobs will simply not exist in twenty years. Can we blame the unions? Or rents and real estate taxes? Of course not. The subsidized productions, sponsored at such museums as New York's Lincoln Center, are not building up a new audience so much as recultivating an old one, since the medium of such drama seems weird and artificial in our new social milieu. We need more portability and flexibility, and this the traditional theater cannot provide. It was made for Versailles and for the sedentary Milords, not for motorized life-demons who travel six hundred miles a week. Versailles no longer speaks very loudly to us, since we think at eighty-five miles an hour.

In the other direction, starting from the idea of theater itself, others such as myself declared war on the script as a set of sequential events. Improvisation was no help; performers merely acted in imitation of a script. So I began to work as if time and sequence could be utterly suspended, not by ignoring them (which would simply be illogical) but by systematically replacing them as structural elements with change. Lack of change would cause my pieces to stop. In 1958 I wrote a piece, *Stacked Deck,* in which any event can take place at any time, as long as its cue appears. The cues are produced by colored lights. Since the colored lights could be used wherever they were put and audience reactions were also cuing situations, the performance-audience separation was removed and a happening situation was established, though less visually oriented in its use of its environment and imagery. At the same time, Al Hansen moved into the area from graphic notation experiments, and Nam June Paik and Benjamin Patterson (both in Germany at the time) moved in from varieties of music in which specifically musical events were frequently replaced by nonmusical actions.

Thus the happening developed as an intermedium, an uncharted land that lies between collage, music and the theater. It is not governed by rules; each work determines its own medium and form according to its needs. The concept itself is better understood by what it is not, rather than what it is. Approaching it, we are pioneers again, and shall continue to be so as long as there's plenty of elbow room and no neighbors around for a few miles. Of course, a concept like this is very disturbing to those whose mentality is compartmentalized. *Time, Life,* and the High Priests have been announcing the death of happenings regularly since the form gained momentum in the late fifties, but this says more about the accuracy of their information than about the liveliness of the form.

We have noted the intermedia in the theater and in the visual arts, the happening, and certain varieties of physical constructions. For reasons of space we cannot take up here the intermedia between other areas. However, I would like to suggest that the use of intermedia is more or less universal throughout the fine arts, since continuity rather than categorization is the hallmark of our new mentality. There are parallels to the happening in music, for example in the work of such composers as Philip Corner and John Cage, who explore the intermedia between music and philosophy, or Joe Jones, whose self-playing musical instruments fall into the intermedium between music and sculpture. The constructed poems of Emmett Williams and Robert Filliou certainly constitute an intermedium between poetry and sculpture. It is possible to speak of the use of intermedia as a huge and inclusive movement of which dada, futurism and surrealism are early phases preceding the huge ground swell that is taking place now? Or is it more reasonable to regard the use of intermedia as an irreversible historical innovation, more comparable for example, to the development of instrumental music than, for example, to the development of romanticism?

1981 In 1965, when the above words were written, the intention was simply to offer a means of ingress into works which already existed, the unfamiliarity of whose forms was such that many potential viewers, hearers, or readers were "turned off" by them. The world was filled at that time with concrete poems, happenings, sound poetry, environments, and other more or less novel developments; unless the public had a way of seeing into the work by causing it to stand still for a moment and be classified, the work was likely to be dismissed as "avant-garde: for specialists only." To any dedicated nonspecialist this could be frustrating—one wanted to know well the art of one's time, since one wanted to hear one's own voice or self at work, without the interventions of history and historical judgments; this was art whose horizons would closely match one's own.

The vehicle I chose, the word "intermedia," appears in the writings of Samuel Taylor Coleridge in 1812 in exactly its contemporary sense—to define works which fall conceptually between media that are already known, and I had been using the term for several years in lectures and discussions before my little essay was written. Furthermore, as part of my campaign to popularize what was known as "avant-garde: for specialists only," to demystify it if you will, I had become a publisher of a small press, Something Else Press (1964–74), which brought out editions of many primary sources and materials in the new arts (as well as reissuing works of the past which seemed to merit new attention—works by Gertrude Stein, the dadaists, the composer Henry Cowell, etc.). It seemed foolish simply to publish my little essay in some existing magazine, where it could be shelved or forgotten. So it was printed as the first *Something Else Newsletter* and sent to our customers, to all the people on our mailing list, to people to whom I felt the idea would be useful (for example, to artists doing what seemed to me to be intermedial work and to critics who might be in a position to discuss such work). All in all, I gave away some ten thousand copies of the essay, as many as I could afford; and I encouraged its republication by anyone who asked for permission to do so. It was reprinted seven or eight times that I knew of, and it still lives on in print in various books, not just of mine, but where it has been anthologized along with other texts of the time or as part of surveys.

The term shortly acquired a life of its own, as I had hoped. In no way was it my private property. It was picked up; used and misused, often by confusion with the term "mixed media." This last is a venerable term from art criticism, which covers works executed in more than one medium, such as oil color and guache. But by extension it is also appropriate to such forms as the opera, where the music, the libretto, and the mise-en-scène are quite separate: at no time is the operagoer in doubt as to whether he is seeing the mise-en-scène, the stage spectacle, hearing the music, etc. Many fine works are being done in mixed media: paintings which incorporate poems within their visual fields, for instance. But one knows which is which.

In intermedia, on the other hand, the visual element (painting) is fused conceptually with the words. We may have abstract calligraphy, concrete poetry, "visual poetry" (not *any* poem with a strong visual element, but the term is sometimes used to cover visual works in which some poem appears, often as a photography, or in which the photographed visual material is presented as a sequence with a grammar of its own, as if each visual element were a word of a sentence, as in certain works by Jean-François Bory or Duane Michaels).

Again, the term is not prescriptive; it does not praise itself or present a model for doing either new or great works. It says only that intermedial works exist. Failure to understand this would lead to the kind of error of thinking that intermedia are necessarily dated in time by their nature, something rooted in the 1960s, like an art movement of the period. There was and could be no intermedial movement. Intermediality has always been a possibility since the most ancient times, and though some well-meaning commissar might try to legislate it away as formalistic and therefore antipopular, it remains a possibility wherever the desire to fuse two or more existing media exists. One can avoid it; one can be like Rosalind Krauss, a much respected critic who said in a lecture at Iowa City in 1981, "I am devoted to the idea of trying to bury the avant-garde," which she does by attacking it, ignoring it and its implications, or, even worse, presenting theory as such an end in itself that any sort of artwork becomes, at best, an unimportant appendage to the theory. But there is always an avant-garde, in the sense that someone, somewhere is always trying to do something which adds to the possibilities for everybody, and that that large everybody will some day follow this somebody and use whatever innovations were made as part of their workaday craft. "Avant-garde" is merely a conventional metaphor drawn (in the mid-nineteenth century) from the military, in which an avant-garde moves in advance of the main body of troops. "Avant-garde" is relative, not absolute. A conservative poet can be at least morally avant-garde by moving in the direction of ever-greater integrity and purity, of vividness or metaphor and excellence of line. Others seek to follow, even when they cannot; and thus the metaphor retains its relevance.

But when one is thinking of the avant-garde of forms and media, one is often thinking of artists who, for whatever reason, question those forms and media. They can reject some (e.g., André Breton's predecessors in French dada rejected the novel, and they were avant-garde, while André Breton chose to move toward some kind of novel as a possibility, thus provoking a break between his group, which in due course became the surrealists, and the other—and the new group, too, was avant-garde). They can create others. And often this creation of new media is done by the fusion of old ones; this was very common in the late 1950s and early 1960s, with the formal fusions I have already mentioned. No work was ever good because it was intermedial; for quality judgments one must look elsewhere. Nor, arguably, was it even timely because of its intermediality.* The intermediality was merely a part of how a work was and is; recognizing it makes the work easier to classify, so that one can understand the work and its significances.

Further, there is a tendency for intermedia to become media with familiarity. The visual novel is a pretty much recognizable form to us now. We have had many of them in the last twenty years. It is harping on an irrelevance to point to its older intermedial status between visual art and text; we want to know what this or that visual novel is about and how it works, and the intermediality is no longer needed to see these things. Same with visual poetry and sound poetry (or "text-sound," if one prefers that term). In the performance arts, once there was the happening which was close to "events"; some happenings artists did fluxus, and some did not. At least one fluxus artist, Alison Knowles, evolved in her work until she found herself doing what other new artists—many of whom took great pains to distinguish what they were doing from happenings, events, and fluxus—were calling, variously, "art performance" or "performance art." Where do we look for to find the continuity of these? To their intermediality:

---

*In 1965 I would have challenged this. But researches into the history of visual poetry and sound poetry have suggested to me that virtually all possible fusions have been made or at least implied at some time or other, and that the surfacing of some volume of such fusions has more to do with the economics or the fashions of a time rather than with its actual *Zeitgeist*.

they are all the same intermedium, a conceptual fusion of scenario, visuality and, often enough, audio elements. But will the intermediality explain the uniqueness or value of the very best of art performance (or performance art)? I think not. Some works will become landmarks and will define their genre, while the others will be forgotten. At best the intermediality was needed to suggest their historical trajectory, to see their sometimes obscure pedigree (as one might use it, with happenings, to point toward the heritage of happenings from dada or futurist manifestations). But if the work is ever to become truly important to large numbers of people, it will be because the new medium allows for great significance, not simply because its formal nature assures it of relevance.

This, then, is the caveat inherent in using the term intermedia: it allows for an ingress to a work which otherwise seems opaque and impenetrable, but once that ingress has been made it is no longer useful to harp upon the intermediality of a work. No reputable artist could be an intermedial artist for long—it would seem like an impediment, holding the artist back from fulfilling the needs of the work at hand, of creating horizons in the new era for the next generation of listeners and readers and beholders to match their own horizons too. What was helpful as a beginning would, if maintained, become an obsession which braked the flow into the work and its needs and potentials. One often regrets the adherence of an artist to a set of dogma: the "movement artist" is a case in point—he adheres to the teachings of his or her movement, long after these have passed their relevance. There is the "late" futurist, the "late" abstract expressionist, the "late" pop artist. To be late in that sense is somehow to create a sort of academicism, good for providing examples to a class ("Okay, class, now this week I want each of you to do a pop art painting"), perhaps useful for heuristic purposes but not likely to open up new horizons for the artist or his viewers, listeners, or readers.

And with this I would leave the matter of intermedia. It is today, as it was in 1965, a useful way to approach some new work; one asks oneself, "what that I know does this new work lie between?" But it is more useful at the outset of a critical process than at the later stages of it. Perhaps I did not see that at the time, but it is clear to me now. Perhaps, in all the excitement of what was, for me, a discovery, I overvalued it. I do not wish to compensate with a second error of judgment and to undervalue it now. But it would seem that to proceed further in the understanding of any given work, one must look elsewhere—to all the aspects of a work and not just to its formal origins, and at the horizons which the work implies, to find an appropriate hermeneutic process for seeing the whole of the work in my own relation to it.

3 The Strategy of Visual Poetry: Three Aspects

As soon as the visual aspect of a poem becomes not just incidental but is actually structural, the strategy of a poem is affected in several ways: (1) the momentum of a linear thrust is broken, since the eye must stop and take note of the shape. A static element is thereby introduced. (2) The idea of the work is less exclusively dependent upon the words of the text and can even become somewhat transcendent to the verbal text. (3) In the case of visual poems which are primarily visual and only lesserly textural—the verbally poetic visual piece—a similar metamorphosis occurs: the verbal aspect becomes transcendent to its visual embodiment, and a kinetic thrust becomes possible in a way that very few visual artworks can have. To make a few beginnings and substantiations of these observations is the purpose of this paper.

The Breaking of the Linear Thrust   Among the traditional thoughts of a poem which a poet tends to keep as a paradigm in his mind is the idea of the poem that "catches you up, and won't let go of you until you have finished reading the poem." In our Western culture this is almost the normative view. It is the source of "power" in a poem. There is an element of compulsion which leads ultimately to catharsis, the touchstone criterion which Aristotle attributed to the tragedies of Sophocles. But Aristotle belonged to a time in Greek culture when it was no longer possible to rest content with the earlier civic virtues and the mental and poetic culture of the previous generation. Greek civilization was becoming obliged to conquer or to be conquered: and the linear philosophy which he developed was geared toward proof and demonstration, ultimately toward power. The aim of his rhetoric is to persuade. The goal of our rhetoric today is far less to persuade than to develop the mental or perceptual resource, to share the experience. Applied to rhetoric, this means that our goal is less to persuade (at least by logical means) than to show in such a way what it feels like to think this or that, what happens if one does think this or that way, and to clothe the thought, therefore, *in the most vivid and memorable embodiment possible* rather than the most logically defensible one. The linear expression of an Aristotelian logic is apt to be left to lawyers: the artists have other concerns.

But the normative taste has been, in poetry, for the powerful poem. The poems that reject this have been damned as decadent, feeble or impotent. Even our occidental lyricism has been power-oriented. As I've noted elsewhere, Shelley's "Ode to a Skylark" seems to be more about a fighter plane than about a bird. Yet each generation must reinvent its arts in its own image; that is the inner drive toward realism, and to go against it can only lead to an art of shallow and hollow gesture. As power is removed from our options, it can be replaced with new criteria that were always there but were undervalued—truth, serenity, harmony. The work which is *forced* to be only one thing, because serious works are thought to be only one thing, may be logically defensible, but it will tend to be experientially inadequate. Thus the drive to make works which are conceptually intermedial—whose essence lies between the traditional media—gathers momentum today as part of a great variety of what passes for "movements" on our cultural scene, though without being a movement in its own right. Many times in history intermedia have appeared—in India following the Hindu revival (and again following the Moslem conquest), in Italy at the end of the Renaissance[1]—and in many other times and places as well. But we see some Italian instances of this drive toward intermedia in the literary and emblematic painting of the late sixteenth century, the many pattern poems of the period (of which more presently), in the emblematic imagery of such works as Giordano Bruno's *Degli Eroici Furori* and in his almost semiotic ideas of syncretic imagery in such later Latin writings as his *De Imaginum, Signorum, et Idearum Compositione* (On the composition of

[1]Dick Higgins, *George Herbert's Pattern Poems: In Their Tradition* (West Glover, Vt.: Unpublished Editions, 1977), pp. 17–19. Hereafter cited as *Higgins* (1977).

images, signs, and ideas) of 1591,[2] and even in the appearance of the opera, which is, however, more of a mixed medium than an intermedium, since there is no conceptual fusion between text, music, and mise-en-scène; the components of a mixed medium remain separate though simultaneous. However, the syncretism of the following quotation from Bruno could equally well serve to describe the theoretical underpinnings of many artists' work since the late 1950s:

Therefore, and in a certain measure, philosophers are painters; poets are painters and philosophers; painters are philosophers and poets. He who is not a poet and a painter is no philosopher. We say rightly that to understand is to see imaginary forms and figures; and understanding is fancy, at least it is not deprived of fancy. He is no painter who is not in some degree a poet and thinker, and there can be no poet without a certain measure of thought and representation.[3]

Thus, returning to the visual poetry of today, it is easy for us to see how the syncretism of a Bruno fits well with the formal syncretism of recent visual poetry and parallel art forms—conceptual art, fluxus performances and happenings, for instance—and indicates the synchronic appropriateness of it, given our cultural milieu. Of course the pattern poem of the past tended to be strongly mimetic—to take the shape of a natural object rather than a geometrical or other schematic form. Figure 1, for instance is a very typical pattern poem of this sort.

Of the roughly 1,100 pattern poems that I have collected from before 1900, probably 85 percent are representational in the sense of the above example, and only about 15 percent are as schematic as the one given in Figure 2, as an example of the other type.

---

[2]Giordano Bruno, *Jordani Bruni Nolani Opere Latine Conscripta*, 3 vols. in 8 pts. (1891; Bad Cannstatt b. Stuttgart, Friedrich Frommann Verlag, 1962), vol. 1, pt. 3, pp. 87–318, esp. 197–99. In collaboration with Charles Doria I am currently working on the first English translation of this text.

[3]Isabel Frith, *Life of Giordano Bruno the Nolan*, ed. Prof. Mauriz Carriere (Boston: Ticknor, 1887), p. 16. What Ms. Frith has done is to assemblé a montage here of passages from the section referred to in fn. 2.

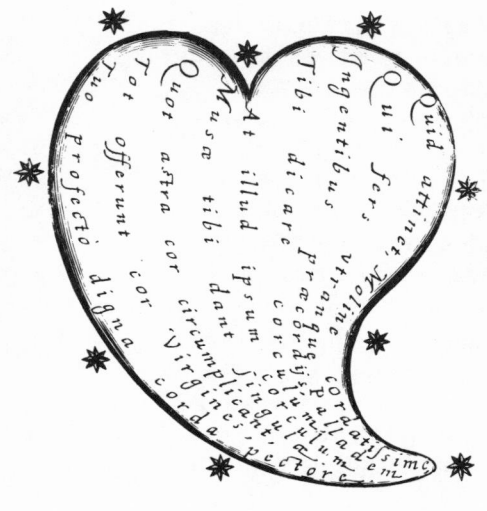

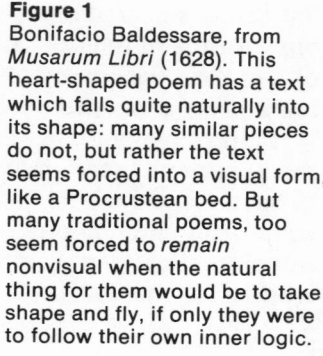

Figure 1
Bonifacio Baldessare, from *Musarum Libri* (1628). This heart-shaped poem has a text which falls quite naturally into its shape: many similar pieces do not, but rather the text seems forced into a visual form, like a Procrustean bed. But many traditional poems, too, seem forced to *remain* nonvisual when the natural thing for them would be to take shape and fly, if only they were to follow their own inner logic.

Figure 2
Amaracandra Sūri, from the *Kāvyakalpalatā* (ca. 1297 A.D.). The Latin Middle Ages abound with cabalistic arrays of letters into grids, moving metatactically from magic into art, whose "inscriptions" can also be rearranged readily into traditional poetry. Several examples will be found in my book on pattern poems, cited in the footnotes. But just to show how universal this phenomenon is, here is an example in Gujarati, an Indian language from the area north of Bombay. This is one of many examples collected by Professor Hiralal R. Kapadia and printed in various issues of the *Journal of the University of Bombay* in 1954 and 1955 and elsewhere. Professor Kapadia gives written-out versions for this text and others, which would otherwise appear to be simply diagrams.

Modern visual poetry tends, however, to be far less mimetic. The visual element is often purely expressive and improvised, in the manner of an abstract expressionist painting. Or it is clean and geometrical. Or its forms are not those of natural objects, but of the ways and processes of nature. Thus the familiar Apollinaire rain calligram shows the words scattered down the page as rain falls, and not spread out into a lattice on the page, as if the falling raindrops could be photographed with a time-stop mechanism. The array of words may be schematic or linguistic; it may resemble the flow charts of a computer programmer's diagram. But what it always does is follow some sort of spatialized method which requires, for the fullest enjoyment of the piece, that we become sensitized to the spatial aspect of the piece. The space is not just a notation, at best a stand-in for time, as is the tendency in traditional poetry. Rather, it is a structural unit which may serve a large variety of purposes.

The Poem Transcends the Verbal Text   Perhaps at this point the concept of metataxis should be introduced. This is a term used in anthropology to describe the shift in function (which determines a shift in identity) of an object from one situation to another. A horse, once a means of transportation, becomes a symbol of status or leisure. A bow and arrow, formerly an instrument of war or a hunting tool, is metatactically altered into being a child's toy. Elsewhere I have pointed out how magical and cabalistic devices, originally intended as metaphors for a hidden truth, became instead metaphors for an aesthetic truth; this explains the art forms of some of the earlier pattern poems.[4] A similar process seems to be involved, as one looks at the role of text in the concrete poems of the 1960s and before, and as one compares them with the *poesia visiva* works of the 1970s.[5] These former usually consisted of arrays of letters or words, while the latter are for more visual than verbal or textual: many consist of photographs of people carrying words or even letters, others show something happening to the words or letters—a process of erasure, metamorphosis, dissolution, or reconstruction.

For anyone who has followed visual poetry or concrete poetry for any length of time, this distinction which I am making between the more text- or letter-oriented sort and the more purely

---

[4]Higgins, 1977.

[5]Christian Wagenknecht, "Proteus and Permutation: Spielarten einer Poetischen Spielart," in *Text + Kritik,* heft 30 (1970), pp. 1–10.

visual variety will come as no surprise. Most of the works in the two major anthologies of the 1960s, those edited by Emmett Williams (*An Anthology of Concrete Poetry,* 1967) and by Mary Ellen Solt (*Concrete Poetry: A World View,* 1968) are of the first sort, while those in more recent books, such as those edited by Jean-Francois Bory (*Once Again,* 1968) and by Klaus Peter Dencker (*Text-Bilder: Visuelle Poesie International,* 1972) include many examples of the latter. A number of the informal magazines devoted to the most visual sort of work have come out of Italy, and so this sort has come to be known by an Italian term for "visual poetry," *poesia visiva.* Some writers such as Klaus Peter Dencker have tried to make a qualitative distinction and a hard line between concrete poetry and "visual poetry" (by which he means *poesia visiva*) and Dencker is currently at work on a large anthology of *poesia visiva* through the centuries—sculptural poems and object poems from the past, up to the most current sort of photographic poems. A hard-line qualitative distinction is, in my opinion, not possible, but a general quantitative one, based on the degree within the intermedial polarity between text or visual orientation, is useful for taxonomic purposes. Anyone who wants to distinguish and verbalize the differences between the concrete or verbal sort, as in the works of Eugen Gomringer, Mary Ellen Solt, the earlier Ian Hamilton Finlay, or Jonathan Williams, and the new works by Finlay (the sailboats), Alain Arias-Misson, or Thomas Ockerse, will find this distinction useful. For those photographic sequence-works of *poesia visiva* that are extremely close to some works of concept art, such as some pieces by Robert Smithson, it is almost impossible to get a sense of text when one reads the work. In a piece by Jean-Francois Bory, one sees photographs of a book left on the send, the tide comes in and bears it away—and it sinks. There may have been words in the book. But does it matter what these were? The criteria for evaluating the nature and impact of such a work are those which would be used for photojournalism or for a performance—in fact, such a work tends to feel like the documentation of a performance which one is to imagine, but

which may or may not have taken place. Not only
the grammar of the text is gone, but the words as
well. Because there is so much of this *poesia
visiva* being done right now, one is apt to forget
that it has been done for a long time. It is nearly
twenty years since Emmett Williams's "Poetry
Clock" (1959) was made; it appeared in his
anthology. And, in a sense and to a degree, many
of the geometric paintings of the Swiss school of
the postwar years, which are historically ancestral
to the term "concrete poetry," can be regarded as
wordless poems. I mean of course paintings by
Richard Löhse, the early Karl Gerstner, and Max
Bill, the last of whom called many of his works
which appeared to be physical realizations
(concretizations?) of an intellectual principle or
progression "Konkretionen," which we would
translate as "concretions." His secretary in the
early 1950s was Eugen Gomringer, to whom the
term "concrete poetry" is usually attributed, and
who used the term by analogy to Bill's works.
Many works by Bill and Löhse and others of that
group consist of series and progressions and even
permutations, and the progressions of shapes or
colors are analogous to the behavior of verbal
elements in what are sometimes referred to as
"Proteus poems" after a famous poem by Julius
Caesar Scaliger. In the paintings, the progression
is one of verbal units. Here are two examples, the
first from Scaliger's "Proteus" (ca. 1561):[6]

> Perfide sperasti divos te fallere Proteu
> Perfide te divos sperasti fallere Proteu
> Perfide te sperasti divos fallere Proteu
> Perfide te Proteu sperasti fallere divos
> Perfide sperasti te divos fallere Proteu

And here is a brief passage from Jackson Mac
Low's "Jail Break (for Emmett Williams & John
Cage) September 1963. April & August 1966:"[7]

> Tear now jails down all.
> Tear all now down jails.
> Tear now all jails down.
> Tear jails now all down.
> Tear jails now down all.

---

[6]Etienne Tabourot, *Les Bigarrures du Seigneur des Accords*
1597/1866: Genève: Slatkine Reprints, 1969), p. 113.

[7]Christian Wagenknecht, "Proteus Und Permutation," in Text &
Kritik.

The relation of such "Proteus poems" to concrete poetry is that what syntax there is is geometric rather than, as in traditional poetry, algebraic—cumulative rather than linear. The elements taken separately have no particular power or impact. But each line gets nearly all its meaning from its relation to the others, where in traditional poetry the lines normally make some sense even when isolated. In a geometric painting, shapes get their relevance from their relation to other shapes, and in a "Proteus poem" the pattern of the components is far more important than just what they happen to be.

In fact, in many cases the pattern is made clearer and more vivid by using elements that relate to words but are not words—numbers, the letters of the alphabet, or visual vocabularies. I made a series of one-of-a-kind (mostly) silk-screen prints using a vocabulary of 300 elements, repeated and juxtaposed in a variety of ways to make almost 900 different works. There is no need for the viewer to see all the works in this series, which is called *7.7.73;* there is just enough information to establish the pattern in a clear and indelible way. Each work in the series is analogous to a line in a poem—and in a "Proteus poem" there is seldom a need to go through every possible line, every possible permutation. The lines of such a work tend to be synecdochal—the parts of the work can stand for the whole. Many of Emmett Williams's pieces in his *Anthology of Concrete Poetry* will serve as examples of the alphabet-poem genre, and the number poems of Richard Kostelanetz or Ladislav Nebesky can illustrate this latter category. Some works of visual art are analogous to these poems—especially certain paintings by Jasper Johns and Robert Indiana. But these latter seem, for the most part, geared to a luxury market and not to the page or the poor connoisseur's library: for social reasons, one would tend, then, to class these last as paintings more than as poems.

The Transcendent Text In the works which I have discussed up to now, the effect has been seen of the introduction of spatial considerations and visual elements into verbal materials, progressively, until their structure is no longer

dependent upon any verbal text, though
something of a verbal method of experiencing the
work remains—the process of reading, of
abstracting a sort of verbal pattern from the work
and subsumption of the visual dimension into that
verbal framework. But of course the opposite is
true too—that there can be visual works whose
impact depends upon their association with the
word, the logos. This is true of many religious
works. There can be a metataxis from a religious
or mystical perception into a political one, as in
the case of the highly emblematic iconography of
many works from the period of the French
Revolution and the Napoleonic era. Or there can
be (and this is what concerns us more here) an
emblematic array of images which embody a
verbal message. In its extreme, this could be the
rebus, taken as an art form (as it was, for instance,
by the French Renaissance poet Clement Marot).
Or it could be simply the emblem literature of the
late Renaissance and baroque, the emblem books
of Francis Quarles and others, or even the works
of William Blake, such as *The Marriage of Heaven
and Hell.* For these, the grammar and pattern of
literature are not superimposed over the visual art
base, necessarily, but rather the verbal image and
often the word itself is included. This would be the
case with a good many advertisting illustrations,
obviously. But it is also the area, conceptually, of
the calligraphic text, the "drawing of words." This
has not been a very productive area for
avant-garde visual poetry, just now. The highest
products of this have been the calligraphic poems
of Paul Reps, or the various collaborations
between abstract expressionist painters and poets
in the 1960s, between Larry Rivers and Frank
O'Hara, for instance. In such work, one tends to
abstract from the whole not so much a reading as
a number of discrete words or images, to notice
the pattern and then let the work go as a whole.
Put linguistically, one sees the *langue*
incompletely because one is not caught up by the
component *paroles.*

Yet, to put the question philosophically, could
there not be a work of this sort which was
independent of the words which comprised it? A
work of pure form, a matrix into which anything

which was put comprised the realization of the work? This is a question which any translator must face: but often it is faced, now, by the artist or poet or concrete poet. How can I "translate" my work from text into music? From one realization of a work into another? In such pieces as *The Twin Plays* (1963) Jackson Mac Low used an identical matrix of action, sentence structure and so on, to make two different stage works; one set of verbal events was made from all the sounds and syllables in the proper name "Port-au-Prince" and the other came from a list of sayings and proverbs recorded in Adams County, Illinois. A similar assumption is at work in Stephen McCaffery's "homolinguistic translations"—systematic puns from given texts to new ones. The potential here for visual poetry is equally great. It seems likely that blank works will come to exist, which one fills with words, and that these will be a new category in visual poetry. Prototypes have been made already by myself and others. Novels which come on cards which one is expected to shuffle and then read aloud (often with materials which the reader also contributes) have some of this character. But as a genre, the area is yet unexplored.

Conclusion Just as one might imagine from the quotation I gave from Giordano Bruno, there are analogous interfaces and intermedia that are similar to the visual poem in poetry/music (sound poetry), poetry/philosophy (concept poetry), even poetry/technology (what Bern Porter calls "sci-art" poems). These too are very much in need of classification, with an accepted taxonomy. It is very difficult to enjoy a work fully before one has made some mental classification of it, and yet the hermeneutics of such classification are very difficult owing to the lack of any consensus. But without the classification, one is ill at ease with a work, unable to relax and live with it. Thus the real need, in understanding visual poetry right now, is not for a dualism of good and bad or true and false, but for an overall teleology of the work which can serve as the basis for both a taxonomy and hermeneutic. For instance, in this paper we have dealt a little with a teleology of visual poetry. But what does this imply for sound poetry? Many sound poems are being distributed on tape cassettes; but one plays a cassette more than once, usually, in a great variety of situations. One hears the cassette at home, and one plays it in one's automobile when one is driving: how does this affect the poem? And in any case, while a traditional poem was made to be witnessed from beginning to end in a book—and was usually designed for its maximum impact to be on first reading (which later readings reevoke), what is the effect of a sound poem in which one assumes the cassette will be played over and over and over again? The text must be designed for reexperiencing. It must "wear well." Similarly, few traditional poems were designed for putting on one's wall and for living with. Yet many visual poems are designed for just that purpose. How does this affect their nature? These are questions which have not yet been answered in any satisfactory way, so far as I know.

But to sum up: the potential for visual poetry lies in its introduction of space and visual shape—at the cost of momentum and kinetic inertia. A visual poem, if it has power, will not gain it from the sequence of verbal images in the same way that Vergil's *Aeneid* did but, rather, in the way that the powerful anti-Hitler graphic photomontages of John Heartfield do. And in any case, the medium seems more suitable for the achievement of lyrical and analytical effects than for the mighty impact that western poetry sought for during the imperial era. We need not be like Joseph Addison, the Aristotelian critic in the eighteenth century, who, in the *Spectator,* denounced all visual poetry as "false wit," because he was unable to see that this loss of power and momentum was accompanied by a holistic realism that would make the visual poetry medium suitable for qualities that he did not associate with poetry. Rather the best strategy for the visual poet consists of matching the natural potentials of the medium (or of the intermedium, depending on how one wishes to look at it) with which ever of his or her notions and projections seem most suited for it, and not to try and force it to do something of which it is not capable. The audience, then, sees this process of matching, identifies it, relaxes and enjoys the process. Which is what happy audiences have always done anyway.

4 Points toward a Taxonomy of Sound Poetry

For Starters, a Subhistory Most sound poets and observers of the contemporary scene approach sound poetry as if it were a purely contemporary phenomenon, but this neoteric view simply does not hold up. It is true that some kinds of sound poetry are new in the sense of being without formal precedent. But just as "concrete" and other recent visual poetries have their analogues going back into folklore or into (for example) the Bucolic Greek poets, so sound poetry too has its close analogues. This is natural, since it is natural for anyone who is interested in poetry to try, at some point, isolating the sounds of poetry from other aspects of it and to try out the making of poems with sounds more or less alone; only if such an experiment were totally artificial could something so basic as a poetry of sound alone be entirely without precedent. But, to start our investigation, let us consider sound poetry not (as might be tempting) by some tight definition that gave a climactic structure to the argument of the critic or poet who offers it—the revelation-of-the-heretofore-unknown-truth kind of discussion—and simply use "sound poetry" as, generally, poetry in which the sound is the focus, more than any other aspect of the work.

Three basic types of sound poetry from the relative past come to mind immediately: folk varieties, onomatopoetic or mimetic types, and nonsense poetries. The folk roots of sound poetry may be seen in the lyrics of certain folk songs, such as the Horse Songs of the Navajos or in the Mongolian materials collected by the Sven Hedin expedition.[1] We have some of this kind of thing in our own culture, where sound-poetry fragments are apt to be used at the ends of stanzas, such as the French "il ron ron ron petit patte à pont" in "Il était une bergère," or the English "heigh down hoe down derry derry down" in "The Keeper," Similarly, in

---

[1]Henning Haslund-Christiansen, *The Music of the Mongols: Eastern Mongolia* (1943; New York: Da Capo Press, 1971).

black American music there is a sound-poetry tradition, possibly based originally on work calls, which we find metastatized into the skat singing styles of the popular music of the 1930s, in the long nonsenselike passages in Cab Calloway's singing of "Minnie the Moocher," for example.

In written literature, by contrast, most of the sound poetry fragments are brief, onomatopoetic imitations of natural or other sounds, for example the "Brekekex ko-ax ko-ax" of the frogs in Aristophanes' drama, or the "jug jug jugs" of the birds among the Elizabethans. This use of sound has no semantic sense to speak of, although, on occasion, its freshness consists of possible overlaps between nonsense and sense. Even some recent sound poetry has an onomatopoetic element. For example, my own *Requiem for Wagner the Criminal Mayor* is above all a structural piece, but its sounds resemble the fighting of cats and also the so-called Bronx cheer of traditional calumny.

Some of the most interesting sound poetry is the purely nonsense writing of the periods in Western literature when nonsemantic styles and forms were not supposed to be taken in full earnest. One of their delights is the art with which they parody the styles of their authors' native tongues. Try this English example, for instance, from the Victorian, Edward Lear:

Thrippsy pillowins,
Inky tinky pobblebookle abblesquabs?—
Flosky! beebul trimple flosky!—Okul scratcha-
bibblebongebo, viddle squibble tog-a-tog,
ferrymoyassity
amsky flamsky ramsky damsky crocklefether squiggs.
                           Flunkywisty poom.
                           Slushypipp.[2]

While not set up as verse and therefore not exactly sound poetry, this text is from the period when prose poems were redeveloped, and it tropes the style of a conventional polite letter of its period quite admirably. Another well-known example

[2]Edward Lear, *The Complete Nonsense Book* (New York: Dodd, Mead, 1934), p. 10.

from its time would be the nonsense words in *Lewis Carroll's* "Jabberwocky"—'Twas brillig in the slithy toves . . ." and that kind of thing. The protagonist is equipped with a "vorpal" sword, and speculation on that kind of sword has been abundant ever since. When I was a child I had a science fiction magazine in my possession—long since vanished—in which two genius children invented a "vorpal" sword to protect themselves against an invasion of creatures from another dimension, and there are currently even a literary magazine in California and an art gallery in New York City named—what else?—*Vorpal.* Thus though no meaning has ever been assigned definitively to "vorpal," the word has become familiar as a sort of empty word, significant for its lack of meaning and for its harmony in a sentence of other, more semantically significant English words.

Similarly, in *Christian Morgenstern's* "Gespräch einer Haussechnecke mit sich selbst," from the famous *Galgenlieder,* a snail asks if it should dwell in its shell, but the word fragments progress and compress into strange, decidely ungrammatical constructs; these use a sort of inner ear and inner grammar of the German language which reveal a great deal about the sounds and potential of that language:

Soll i aus meim Hause raus
Soll i aus meim Hause nit raus?
Einen Schritt raus?
Lieber nit raus?
Hausenitraus—
Hauserans
Hauseritraus
Hausenaus
Rauserauserauserause . . .[3]

which *Max Knight* has translated as follows:

Shall I dwell in my shell?
Shall I not dwell in my shell?
Dwell in shell?
Rather not dwell?
Shall I not dwell,
shall I dwell,

[3]Christian Morgenstern, *The Gallows Songs* (Berkeley: University of California Press, 1966), pp. 28–29.

dwell in shell
shall I shell,
shalllshelllshalllshelllshalll . . .

Of course in German the last five words can be
perfectly compressed into one invented word
each, which cannot be done to the same extent in
English. This illustrates not only the uniqueness of
the German language but also the unique
relationship between successful sound poetry and
the effective use of the linguistic potentialities in
any given language.

**When Sound Poetry Becomes Conscious of Itself
as Just Another Genre** At some point around the
time of the First World War it ceased to be
assumed that sound poetry could only be used for
light or humorous works or as interludes in
otherwise traditional pieces, or as something so
unique that each poem appeared to be the first
sound poem in history—assumptions that seem to
underlie most early sound poems. The sense of
pioneering was replaced by the sense of potential
mastery, and a tradition of sound poetry was
precipitated. Implicit in this development is the
even more radical aesthetic shift which seems to
have begun at this time (and to have become even
more pronounced recently, since, say, the late
1950s) that it is no longer *de rigeur* that a poem
must attempt to be powerful, meaningful, or even
necessarily communicative (a main assumption of
the eighteenth and nineteenth century poetries). I
have developed this observation more fully
elsewhere,[4] but basically my argument is that
poetries which used means which, while not
unknown, were not usually taken seriously in the
West, especially visual as well as sound poetry,[5]

---

[4]I have developed this argument more fully in three parts of
Dick Higgins, *A Dialectic of Centuries: Notes towards a Theory
of the New Arts.* 2d ed. (New York: Printed Editions, 1979), pp.
xi, 3–9, 93–101, and also in Dick Higgins, *George Herbert's
Pattern Poems: In Their Tradition* (New York: Printed Editions,
1977), pp. 18–19.

[5]The early history of visual poetry is my subject in the work
listed in fn. 4, above. Its bibliography will also be useful for
anyone seeking to explore the matter farther. For a similar
discussion of sound poetry, but one which continues into
modern times as well, the best such article in English is that of
Stephen Ruppenthal and Larry Wendt, "Vocable Gestures: A
Historical Survey of Sound Poetry," in *Art Contemporary* 5

could now be accepted as valid possibilities and genres.[6] Thus the *parole in libertà* (1909) of the futurist T. F. Marinetti or the dada *lautgedichte* of Hugo Ball (1917), both of which flourished at this time and both of which, while they may include elements of humor, are not particularly intended as *divertissements* as is, for instance, the Edward Lear piece I cited. The cycle since then is a sort of arc of increasing acceptance of these genres as our mentality has shifted from the normative art of power in the late nineteenth century toward an art of experience and paradigm today. As a measure of just how much a Ball *lautgedicht* (a work which probably seemed quite esoteric at the time of its composition) is accepted, one can point to the use of Ball's "I Zimbra" in its surprising appearance as the lyrics to a recently popular song by the punk rock group, The Talking Heads.[7] The punk rock song, like Ball's poem, opens with "Gadji bera bimba clandridi," which is not even anchored in the parody of any *one* language but is purely without reference to *any* known language. This in turn evokes the possibility of an artificial invented language, an idea which was also explored at this same time in the Russian Iliazd's "zaoum" or the German Stefan George's "lingua romana" pieces. In our taxonomy, then, works in an artificial or nonexistent language will be the first class of modern sound poems.[8]

A second class comprises works in which the joy or other significance of the work lies in the interplay between the semantically meaningful lines or elements and those which are probably nonsense. It is thus related to the first class, and such pieces often use found materials collaged

---

(1978); 57–8, 80–104. A large study of the subject by Henri Chopin was recently published in France, which should help fill in the gap in historical scholarship in sound poetry.

[6]For an example of a naive attack on visual poetry, see Hippolyte Taine, *History of English Literature* (New York: Holt & Williams, 1872), 4:54. Another such attack is in Joseph Addison, *Spectator* 58, many editions.

[7]The Talking Heads' "I Zimbra" is on their album, *Fear of Music* (New York: Sire Records, 1979), SRK 6076.

[8]Many excellent examples of such work are given in Eugene Jolas, "From Jabberwocky to *Lettrisme*" in *Transition Forty-Eight* (1948), v. 1, n. 1, pp. 104–120.

into the text, as it were, so that one gets either a shock of recognition or a momentarily heightened sense of immediate, concrete reality. These works parallel, conceptually, the early collages of Picasso or Braque with their inclusion of newspaper fragments among the forms on the canvas, or the use of photographs by the dadaists and such Bauhaus figures as Moholy-Nagy, or the *objets trouvés* of Marcel Duchamp. That traditional critics can still be puzzled by such works is indicated by the titles of the contributions to a 1972 issue of *Text+Kritik* devoted to the writings of Kurt Schwitters, the German near-dadaist who flourished in the 1920s and later. Sample titles: "Kurt Schwitters' Poem 'To Anna Blume': Sense or Nonsense?" or "On the Function of the Reality Fragments in the Poetry of Kurt Schwitters," etc.[9] Another such device, though not one that fits into sound poetry, would be the "newsreel" passages of John Dos Passo's *USA* trilogy, which I only mention as a parallel paradigm.

A third class might be called "phatic poems," poems in which semantic meaning, if any, is subordinate to expression of intonation, thus yielding a new emotional meaning which is relatively remote from any semiotic significance on the part of words which happen to be included. If, for example, one were to wail the words "blue" and "night" repeatedly over a period of time, the initial function of those words to establish a frame for the wail would soon become unimportant by comparison with the musicality of the wail itself and residual meaning of the two words would come to seem more like an allusion than a conveyor of meaning. One would have, in effect, an invocation without anything specific being invoked. This is precisely the effect which one gets from the recently re-discovered recording by Antonin Artaud of his "Pour en finir avec le jugement de dien," which was originally recorded in the late 1940s a short time before the poet's death, broadcast (causing a great scandal), and then lost for many years until Arrigo Lora-Totino unearthed it in the archives of Radiodiffusion

---

[9]*Text+Tritik 35*–36: (1972), 13 and 33.

Francaise.[10] Here Artaud uses more or less conventional words, but they are, as I have suggested, essentially allusions—or perhaps illusions, since so few can be understood anyway. Instead Artaud's emphasis is on high sighing, breathing, wheezing, chanting, exclaiming, exploding, howling, whispering, and avoiding.

Poems without written texts constitute a fourth class. They may have a rough schema or notation that is akin to a graphic musical one (and there are those who regard a magnetic tape as a sort of notation), or there may be some general rules, written out like those of a game, which, if followed, will produce a performance of the work. But by comparison with the role of the written text and the heard result in traditional poetry or in the previous sound poetries that we have discussed (except, perhaps, the previous class, the phatic poems), they are relatively unnotated. Highlights in this class would be Henri Chopin's explorations of the voice by means of microphone and tape recorder, François Dûfrène's very phatic *crirhythmes* series (which, perhaps, constitute a transitory class between the phatic poems and the unwritten-out ones), or the highly sophisticated tape recorded poems produced in the recording studio by such artists as the Swedes, Bengt Emil Johnson, Sten Hanson, and others.[11] A very large portion of the recorded literature of sound poetry, especially in Europe, is of this type, presumably because of the inherent close connection between such works and audio recording as an industry. Although this is also the class in which most American sound poetry falls, the American literature tends to be aesthetically naïve by comparison to the European (and Canadian) works. The artists seem ill at ease with the very "performance" of their "texts." For example, there

---

[10]Arrigo Lora-Totino, ed., *Futura/Poesia Sonora* (Milano: Cramps Records, 1979), 5206 304. This seven-record set contains a large program book with many materials that are unavailable elsewhere.

[11]Recordings of highlights of seven of the International Sound Poetry Festivals, held at Stockholm from 1968 to 1975, can be found on five records from Sveriges Radios Förlag, RELP 1049 1054 1072 1073 and 1074, and on two from Fylkingen Records, RELP 1102 and 1103.

are some ten records in the Poetry Out Loud series, edited by Peter and Patricia Harleman, which seem somehow like an extension of the beat poetry of the 1950s with its heavy jazz influence, its antiformal bias, and its dogmatic insistence upon the freshness of improvisation.[12] There exist also similar records edited and produced independently by John Giorno, whose work tends to sound improvised even when it is not. These have isolated fragments of rich material, but most are heavy-handed in their unformed iconoclasm. Fortunately, even in America, there are exceptions such as the works of Jackson Mac Low, Richard Kostelanetz, and Charles Stein, which are not of this sort.

The fifth class is the notated sound poem, which comprises the largest volume of sound poetry to date. By "notation" here I am referring to the normative sort of musical notation, in which there is some kind of correspondence between space, time, word, and sound and some form of graphic or textual indicator of those elements. Some of these notations closely resemble musical notations and have elaborate scores, such as the work in the 1940s of the *lettriste* Isidore Isou or the monumentally complex works that came out of Germany in the 1950s, such as Hans G. Helms's *Golem* or Ludwig Harig's *Das Fussballspiel Ein Stereophonisches Börspiel,* a page of which is reproduced herewith:

However, it could also be argued that any *text,* when it is taken as a work of art by a person who does not understand the meaning of its words, is conceptually transformed into a sound poem of this class. For example, in February 1960, during a now-legendary performance of some "happenings" at New York's Judson Church, Claes Oldenburg (who later became celebrated as a pop artist) read aloud to his American audience from a Swedish translation of *The Scarlet Pimpernel.* Since Oldenburg's Swedish is excellent, what the audience heard was all the phatic and phonetic materials of the Swedish language. Once the

---

[12]*Poetry Out Loud* (St. Louis, Mo.: Out Loud Productions, 1971 to 1977).

Harig's *Das Fussballspiel* ("The Soccer Game) is, as its cover proclaims, "a stereophonic radio play," the word for which is, in German, appropriately enough, "hörspiel" or "hear-play." The resources called for on the depicted page alone are one chorus which evidently is working in unison here with a second and third chorus a man and a woman. The work was first broadcast by Südwestfunl in Stuttgart on April 11, 1966 (Ludwig Harig, *Das fussbalspiel: Ein Stereophonisches Hörspiel [Stuttgart: Edition Hansjörg Mayer, 1967]*).

spectator gave up trying to understand the semantic meaning of the words, the result was fresh and meaningful on another plane.

Another such development is the use of a work which was presumably designed for an experience in some other medium in poetry, to produce a sort of intermedial translation. For example, there is the intertextual and intermedial relationship of sound poetry and concrete poetry. Concrete poetry is, quite roughly, the genre of visual poetry which uses writing or the letters of the alphabet presented visually or systematically, as opposed to visual poems which are photographic, environmental, conceptual, temporal, etc.[13] Concrete poetry became a widespread phenomenon in the late 1950s and 1960s. However, occasionally the need to perform concrete poetry "live would arise. So when the poets would be asked to read their work aloud, they would often use the printed texts by analogy to musical notations, thus transforming them into notated sound poems. So close is the connection between sound poetry and concrete poetry, in fact, that many artists have done both and, in fact, one of the first phonographic recordings of sound poetry as such, the 1966 *Konkrete Poesie/Sound Poetry/Artikulationen,* by its very title indicates the near-identity of sound and concrete poetry; some of the artists included, such as Ernst Jandl, Franz Mon, and Lily Greenham, are known in both areas, and Ms. Greenham has toured in Europe and North America with her live performances of concrete poetry translated into sound poetry.[14]

Finally, within this fifth class there is another hybrid, sound poems which are also radio plays, or which seemed designed to be heard not as a unique experience but as part of something else, so that the sound of the words is accompanied by the meanings from some different area of experience. One hears the text with only half one's attention, as one hears most radio broadcasts with only half one's attention; this is more or less inherent in the nature of radio, that one plays it

---

[13]I say "roughly" because, for purposes of discussion, I am agnoring that subgenre of concrete poetry which is either calligraphic or is written in nonlegible writing. Many fine anthologies of concrete poetry have appeared. For example, one of the largest, one which is technically out of print but which is often found, is Emmett Williams, ed., *An Anthology of Concrete Poetry* (New York: Something Else Press, 1967).

[14]Anastasia Bitzos, ed., *Konkrete Poesie/Sound Poetry/Artikulationen* (Bern: Anastasia Bitzos, 1966). Ms. Bitzos produced at least one other such record as well. There also are several records of Lily Greenham's sound-poetry translations of concrete, for example: *Internationale Sprachexperimente der 50/60er Jahre/International Language Experiments of the 50/60ies* [sic] (Frankfurt am Main: Edition Hoffmann, ca. 1970). Unfortunately there exists, as yet, nothing like a comprehensive discography of sound poetry.

Taxonomy of
Sound Poetry
49

while watering the house plants, while driving through heavy traffic, or while sorting out the addresses in one's address book. My own *Le petit cirque au fin du monde* and *Ommaje* are of this subclass. The first is a "hear-play" written in French, a language I do not speak well, so that the errors in it are part of its texture, and it was broadcast repeatedly over the public address system at the University of Vincennes by Jean-Jacques Lebel's students during the May 1968 insurrection in France, a perfect environment for that piece.

These, then, are the five relatively modern classes of sound poetry: (1) works in an invented language, (2) near-nonsense works, (3) phatic poems, (4) unwritten-out poems, and (5) notated ones. Obviously some of the modern works being generated today still fall within the three classes I described earlier in older sound poetry: (1) folk varieties, (2) onomatopoetic or mimetic pieces, and (3) nonsense poetries which trope their own languages. For example, there is no doubting the modernity or avant-garde credentials of the Toronto-based group, The Four Horsemen, whose members perform both separately and together. In their performances they allude constantly to folk or popular culture, to the extent of wearing the kind of elaborate, almost psychedelic clothes associated with rock and roll groups—and they even trope the style of rock and roll to the point of listening to each other take riffs and solos and playing off each other as any tight rock group would. Their presentations are deliberately popular and light-spirited in order to minimize the gulf that usually exists between performer and audience in the new arts. Yet, formally this work belongs to two of the oldest of sound poetry traditions—the folk and nonsense traditions. In no way does this work to the detriment of their achievement, but rather it serves to remind us of something very deep within us which sound poetry expresses clearly when it is at its best—the love of the sound of poetry.

Some Boundaries and Nonboundaries of Sound Poetry Now that we have examined some eight classes of things that sound poetry is, it might be fruitful to turn our attention briefly to some things that sound poetry eigher is not, or is not *yet.*

One thing that sound poetry is not is music. Of course it has a musical aspect—a strong one. But if one compares typical sound poetry pieces with typical musical ones, music is usually the presentation or activization of space and time by means of the occurrences of sound. This is the nature of the most traditional Mozart piano pieces or Irish unaccompanied airs as of the most innovative John Cage musical inventions. But *any* poetry relates space, time, and sound to experience. Thus sound poetry points in a different direction, being inherently concerned with communication and its means, linguistic and/or phatic. In implies subject matter; even when some particular work is wholly nonsemantic, as in the microphonic vocal explorations of Henri Chopin, the nonsemantic becomes a sort of negative semantics—one is conscious of the very absence of words rather than, as in vocal music, merely being aware of the presence of the voice. Thus, for the sound poet certainly and probably for the audience as well, the creation or perception of a work as sound poetry has to do with questions of meaning and experience which are not essentially musical. We identify what we are hearing more than we would if we were listening to music. We are very concerned with just who or what is saying or doing what.

Some of the things that sound poetry has not yet become are intermedial. Intermedia are those formal, conceptual areas of the arts which fall between already accepted media, such as visual poetry falling between the visual arts and poetry. However there is always a tendency for intermedia, experienced with increasing familiarity, to become themselves new media. Thus, taking sound poetry no longer as an intermedium but as a medium, it would be exciting if the sound poets would explore these three new intermedia: (1) those between sound poetry and linguistic analysis; (2) those between sound poetry and sculpture, to produce profoundly three-dimensional poetic constructs and not merely analytical ones; and (3) those between sound poetry and the environment.

In the first of these new intermedia, we could use electronic means to apply the analyzed sounds of one language to the conceptual structure of another to see what aesthetic effects would be made possible. We could write English with the transformations of German. We could generate new categories of what the linguists have called "illegal" sentences—sentences that have no possible correspondences in the physical world (e.g., Noam Chomsky's famous "colorless green ideas sleep furiously"). All sorts of new macaronics would be worth exploring—puns and mixtures among different languages, not to be humorous but to expand our experiences.

In the second new intermedium poems would appear in situations and points of space, and would move toward other situations and points of space in an exciting way. Masses of sound and word, physical presence of more words—these things would enable new poetic structures to enter into our experience.

Finally, the third intermedium could exist in environments and situations which we do not normally regard as poetic. We could have poems for sauna baths, for sunsets, for the experiencing of elections from among the apple trees. We could use aspects of those places that would aestheticize our relationships to them, as traditionally, a prayer was supposed to spiritualize our relationship to its circumstances—a prayer for nighttime, a prayer for those who were lost at sea. There is a lot to be done in these areas and more.

5 Music without Catharsis

In the first part of this century what seemed to be the most striking development was the liberation of the tonal dissonance, the concept that dissonances need not be resolved into consonances; the disappearance of a tonal center and its replacement by a constantly evolving chromatic movement was certainly a current which led from Beethoven and some of his antecedents through Wagner, reaching its apogee in Schoenberg, Hauer, and Ives, to mention only a few obvious instances. But by the 1930s this tendency had evolved to its logical extremes and had become a resource which was no longer particularly innovative; it reached its stage in due course where, for example, Theodor Adorno, certainly one of the most acute critics of the time, would insist on dogmatic grounds that a flaw with the music of Mahler, Schoenberg's champion and, to some extent, master or teacher, was that it tended to be too diatonic, to reject the (to Adorno) obvious role of dissonance.

In the mid-century the task appeared to be twofold, and there was probably no doubt it was something which needed to be done: the inclusion of noise and the rejection of what had become an excess of cerebral structure, an overrational current. The masters in this direction would be Edgard Varèse and John Cage, the former of whom opened up the way for sounds that were not traditionally considered musical, for example the sounds of the sirens in his *Ionization,* to become the focus of musical experience. Not just percussion music as such but also found sounds entered into the act. Concurrent with this was the replacement of rational structure by elements of chance, sometimes systemic and sometimes random in other ways. The process of opening the door to noise was not, of course, without its precedents; futurist music (Russolo) and the music of the Russian constructivists (Mossolov and others) had provided paradigms in this direction before the percussion ensembles of Cage and Lou Harrison, among others, had been founded. Furthermore, even in the works of Schoenberg there are nuclei of thought in this direction in the concept of the *Klangfarbenmelodien* (melodies of timbre) in such works as the *Herzgewächse Kantate.* Fluxus music in the early 1960s brought this to one of its logical extremes, when the nature of the sounds was so flexible that the focus of the music began to lie elsewhere, in the actions taken to produce such pieces—the action music of Nam June Paik and others. A parallel notion is the idea of the musical snapshot—tape-recorded pieces from the environment, for example, as done by Luc Ferrari and the *musique concrète* group.

But in all these tendencies, though less so in the works of Cage himself, whose philosophy militated against it, the overall purpose of the music was to produce a powerful impression, one designed to achieve a catharsis on the part of the listener. Yet one of the clear currents, as we can see at the end of the twentieth century, is the decline of the Aristotelian assumptions which had monitored almost all of Western art since the end of the baroque; and starting in the 1950s this was nowhere more clear than in the decline of catharsis as an implicit assumption of the teleology or purpose of our arts.

The dissatisfaction with catharsis in music is seen already in the 1930s in the surrealist critique of music in general, with the valid perception that by its intensity of emotional involvement that it tended to produce appetites which it could not even begin to satisfy, that it was analogous to a drug or an opiate, leading the listener into realms of dependence which militated against the perception of both daily reality and even of a holistic aesthetic vision.

Furthermore, there were lyrical currents in music even in the nineteenth century—for example, in many songs of Schubert or pieces by Chabrier and Verdi—in which vision replaced catharsis as the aim; the listener was to be swept up in a melodic current rather than an emotional one. The apogee of such lyric involvement is perhaps Erik Satie, whose music was puzzling or trivial to most of his contemporaries and immediate successors, and whose importance and reputation have increased in the wake of the decline of this Aristotelian assumption of catharsis as a goal. I think one can also safely predict that the works of Hauer, who florished in the early part of this century and who totally rejects catharsis as an aim, and who seemed somehow to languish in the shadow of Schoenberg (to whom his methodology of twelve-tone composition has some superficial resemblance), will assume increasing importance with the decline of these assumptions.

Joseph Matthias Hauer (1883–1959) is indeed a fascinating figure in the decline of the role of catharsis and its replacement by a more lyrical or spiritual one; most of his music follows the beat of the human pulse, is to be played at moderate volume, has neither melogy nor consistent harmonic development to sustain it, and listening to it is an experience somehow akin to watching the play of a fountain, so naturally it flows and so lyrically, with only the barest minimum of timbral or rhythmic shift. Its quality is similar, perhaps, to those Indian classical works where serenity is the assumption and in which, if there is a climax at all, one only recognizes it by its quickening of pace. In fact Cage and Harrison both have drawn heavily on oriental models, the latter technically and formally, and the former philosophically, studying Zen philosophy with Daisetz T. Susuki, the results of which can be heard in such works as the incredibly serene *String Quartet* of the late 1940s.

But what of other models?

One style which developed in the 1960s has been called "modular music," music developed around the principle of modules or small repeated patterns of melody; these differ from the traditional ostinatos of music, which are also repeated melodic fragments, in that these latter are usually used to accompany the rest of the composition. When one is working with the modular style, one takes these modules and focuses upon a sequence of them, changing them rather slowly, dropping one out and introducing another to create what is overall a music of texture. Some of the composers who have used this style extensively are Terry Riley, Philip Glass,

Frederic Rzewski, La Monte Young, Steve Reich, and, in England, Michael Nyman. Within the modular style a rather large range of aesthetics is possible. For example, Rzewski's music is a sort of political expressionism. Young is an eclectic, self-consciously employing sources from Indian, Balkan, and jass musics, reflecting on these without originating anything of his own. Riley and Glass strive for a hypnotic effect, using fragments with maximum torque, often building to psychological climaxes which are indeed cathartic. This gives their music a compelling effect that is, at best, hypnotic, but which indeed opens up the way to a critique of the surrealist sort which I mentioned earlier, that such music is an opiate, with all the problems which this entails. In fact the psychedelic movement of the 1960s exactly coincided with the beginnings of this music and it now appears, to some extent, to reflect the drug culture of the time.

But the most rigorous of the modular composers was and is Steve Reich. Some of his pieces do have a catharsis-oriented climax. One of the more fascinating of his pieces is "Come Out," in which he takes a phrase, spoken by a black man in describing a situation of police violence; Reich repeats it, alters it electronically, and accumulates it up to the point of a shattering climax. But other of his pieces function quite differently, remaining cool and structure-oriented, and these pieces, such as the early "Variations on Some Watermelons" (which takes its name from a popular song) or the more recent "Music for 18 Musicians," resist all temptation to blur or to dazzle. The modules are rhythmic as well as melodic, and the listener is stimulated by the shifts in instrument and timbre rather than dazed by them. Climaxes exist in Reich's music, but they are quite often noncathartic, in what they are less psychological climaxes than structural ones—tutti, where all the instruments are playing at once—they seem natural enough as, simply, the points of densest sound and, psychologically, they function as a point of refreshment analogous to silence. The use of sound to frame silence, or of silence to frame sound, is of course a familiar one; the principle of this is as old as human thought, being implicit in Lao-tse's *Tao Te Ching* (ca. 560 B.C.) where he repeatedly points out that to know the black, we must also know the white and vice versa—each absolute is only comprehensible in terms of its potential opposite, and therefore implies the potential of changing to its opposite as well. Listening to music which has climaxes of this sort, we often experience the same kind of serenity in the climaxes which we experience in the silences, and this is a very different experience from that of the climaxes in Aristotelian, psychological art. There is no manipulation of the listener's presumed emotional trajectory (usually drawn from the composer's use of his own passions as reference) such as we find in nineteenth-century symphonies.

Cage's music of the 1950s, with its aleotoric methodology and perhaps ideology, is such a strong statement that it is often taken as a point of reference, with other developments that have happened subsequently categorized as "Post-Cagean." If that be so, then we should at least take notice of the fact that one of the most important Post-Cagean composers is Cage himself. Some of his recent pieces use the production of sound by such indirect methods that the performer himself cannot tell is his action will produce a sound or not; for example, he has used a team of performers with conch shells which are wired for sound and amplified, and into which water has been put. The interior structure of the shells is such that a performer's action may or may not cause the water to shift, thus causing a sound to occur. The sound is then amplified. Clearly using such a musical instrument one is at a yet farther stage from Aristotelian emotional manipulativeness.

I have already mentioned fluxus, the history of which is already available elsewhere.[1] Without

---

[1]There is no comprehensive source of information on fluxus at this time (1981), but some useful texts are Dick Higgins, *Postface* (New York: Something Else Press, 1964); Harry Ruhé, *Fluxus: The Most Radical Art Movement of the 1960's* (Amsterdam: Gallery A, 1980), primarily an information source on some fluxus artists, it also lists excellent bibliographic materials; Hanns Sohm, *Happenings and Fluxus* (Köln: Kölner Kunstverein, 1970).

attempting to define fluxus, which is a sort of nonmovement, an attitude of iconoclasm and constant change in all the arts, it still seems necessary to point out a few of the characteristic methodologies which fluxus composers have employed, all of which are noncathartic in their orientation:

1. Many pieces work "by intention"—the composer gives a set of rules or parameters, and the performers, following these rules in public in live time, cause the audience or spectators to experience the piece. This is a method used very extensively by Philip Corner, Alison Knowles, myself, and many others.
2. Other pieces are extremely minimal—the composer mentions some materials, and what is done with them constitutes the performance. This method has been used by George Brecht, Robert Watts, and others. The extreme brevity discourages climaxes.
3. A third kind of piece uses a simple, formal, and logical progression of some kind, and the performers work out the method of realizing it; often it is presented as a graphic configuration with no method of interpreting it. My "Graphis 24" (1959)[2] is of this sort. This class of piece has been done even more extensively by a nonfluxus artist, Tom Johnson, of whom more will be heard presently.

Graphic notations are a means of describing what is to happen—its configurations suggest the musical events which will occur, or they describe the overall matrix of the piece which the performers then fill in. The advantages of composing in this way are twofold: (1) By setting a general parameter for the performance, without calling for specific materials, the performer is free to do whatever he or she does best, to take the fullest advantage of his or her own skills. (2) By causing the performer to respond to graphic indications as opposed to improvisation, one problem inherent in improvisation is avoided, namely the tendency of the performer to follow a

[2]A detailed account of my Graphis series, with many illustrations, is in the following book: Dick Higgins, *foew&ombwhnw* (New York: Something Else Press, 1969).

psychological track based on the limitations of his or her own experience, taste, and psychology, which usually would lead to very conventional and unadventurous results. Graphic notations were pioneered by Cage in such works as the *Piano Concert* (1957), but other composers of a great variety of orientations have used them—Robert Moran, Anastis Logothetis, Earle Brown (some of whose graphic notations antecede those of Cage), Philip Corner, Malcolm Goldstein, myself, and many others.[3]

Now, to turn from methods to people, a few names might be mentioned as paradigmatic: Charlie Morrow, Pauline Oliveros, and Philip Corner.[4] Corner studied in the 1950s with Messaien, and in the 1960s at Columbia University, then a center of ultrarational, post-Webernite composition, on the one hand, and of extreme neoromanticism, both of which, however, he rejected. He was on the edge of fluxus—a small number of his works were performed in fluxus concerts—but mostly he remained independent, since his orientation was toward highly complex, rather large-scale pieces. When he was in Korea with the U.S. Army he studied oriental calligraphy, and many of his notations are graphic and calligraphic. A selection of his works of this time was published in *The Four Suits* (New York: Something Else Press, 1966) and some of his more recent pieces have been published by Edition Peters, so his work is readily available. Three kinds of work are most characteristic of him:

1. Compositions by intention, in which he describes verbally the sonic or theatrical

---

[3]The most useful survey of (then) contemporary musical and performance notations is the following: John Cage, *Notations* (New York: Something Else Press, 1968). It does not, however, have explanations of how these notations are to be used.

[4]I have mentioned almost only Americans because I am most familiar with their work, but obviously noncathartic music is a worldwide development, and there are many European and Japanese composers equally deserving of attention. Especially with regard to the Japanese, so little information is available in English that we very much need a book on the Japanese contemporary music scene, in order that these composers' ideas can enter into the worldwide flow of musical commonalities.

procedures necessary to perform his works: follow the rules and a performance results;
2. Graphic notations in which the calligraphy suggests the texture which we wants to achieve;
3. Meditations on a sound or an instrument, such as the recent Elementals series or the *Metal Meditations.*[5]

The overall structure of his pieces is "organic" in that it follows either something inherent in the kind of materials which he is using, or that it follows life patterns more than some preconceived formal pattern.

Pauline Oliveros is in some ways similar to Philip Corner in that she too works by intention, but the graphic element in her work is minimal; one of her most notable series is "sonic meditations," which are pure meditations, not necessarily on some specific sound but also on the context of sounds. Her forms often are preconceived and are highly complex and pageantlike, resembling live mandalas. The theatrical element in her work is very strong (but not cathartic), even in such pieces as *In Memoriam Marilyn Monroe and Valerie Solanis,* an orchestral work which ends in total darkness. Another notable piece is *El Relicario de los Animales,* a procession of singers and instruments imitating the sounds of animals. Her textures are apt to be very rich and opulent.

Charlie Morrow brings a craft approach to his compositions rather than a philosophical one. His most notable series are, perhaps: (1) a series of chants, which he improvises for certain settings such as the solstices of the year, dawn, or specific situations, in which he puts himself into a trance and sings with a small gong to tie him to reality; (2) a series of works to be performed in nature, such as a memorable piece for spring frogs; (3) a series of pageants for masses of instruments, such as *Wave Hill* for forty cellos, a similar piece for enormous numbers of trumpets, and so on. There

[5]A spectacular portfolio of Corner's *Metal Meditations* was published in Asolo, Italy, by Francesco Conz in 1979, and a phonograph record of it is due to be released in the near future by René Block in Berlin, Germany. Besides works published by Edition Peters, many of Corner's works are available through Printed Editions, P.O. Box 27, Barrytown, N.Y. 12507 (USA).

is something very healthy feeling about Morrow's pieces—a wholesome physicality, a sense of humor and irony and simplicity; one never has the feeling in his work which one finds in so many avant-garde composers of a lesser stature, that what you are hearing is an academic etude intended to prove some point. Instead, the work is the goal for its own sake.

A younger composer who should be mentioned as representing a different kind of noncathartic orientation is Tom Johnson, who uses his music as a way of making manifest formal ideas, such as geometric progressions and structures. His is probably the most rational music ever devised. For example, he will hang a set of rows or bells to form a square, then walk from one point to the next, ringing the bells in various sequences, until all the basic patterns have been exhausted. The result is, at its best, a quite delightful ritual; what it tends to lack in emotional depth it makes up in appealing pattern and design. One feels that one has been looking at a kaleidoscope, and the hearer/viewer gets into the act, trying to guess what the next pattern will be.

These composers do not form a school in any sense. When we hear music by Schoenberg's followers, we usually can identify them by their dissonant counterpoint and irregular rhythms as members or followers of the so-called Second Viennese School more readily than we can identify their works by individual styles. But no clear-thinking listener would ever confuse works by Corner with those by Oliveros, Morrow, or Johnson. They are merely a collection of individuals with some techniques and a noncathartic purpose in common.

Is anything similar happening in the other arts? Yes, there are related developments in dance and in some recent sound poetry. The works of such dancers as Trisha Brown often follow patterns that are not far from those of Tom Johnson. Meredith Monk has, on occasion (as in the dance *Juice*), used forms of pageantry that are not far from Oliveros's music. And most of the sound poems by John Cage (e.g., *Empty Words*) and Jackson Mac Low seem like rituals in which spoken materials appear and disappear instead of people or instruments. In other words, what we have here is an aesthetic trend rather than one which is solely confined to music.

But what then are some purposes in an aesthetic of this sort? In an art which employs catharsis, Aristotle says in his *Poetics,* the purpose is to purge the spectator of harmful passions; if one consciously avoids catharsis as an aim, what is left?

One answer is that such arts can draw the listener or spectator or viewer into an active relationship with his or her own daily reality. The composer presents a vision of possible sounds, which is his or her horizon of musical experience. At times the composer works directly with the audience, either using the audience as performer or by presenting the materials of the performance directly as a sound environment. At other times the composer uses a performer as medium or as model, communicating with the performer by means of a notation which draws the performer into the creative process (rather than, as in traditional notations, presenting a definitive and explicit statement). The audience then witnesses the process of realization. Each member of the audience has his or her own horizons, according to each member's role in his or her private life, past cultural experience, and so on. The horizons then fuse; in Hans-Georg Gadamer's terminology, there is a *Horizontverschmelzung.* And the audience is, then, drawn into the creative process. This is not music for closing your eyes to, and being swept along in a tide of passion. This is music for the wideawake and active. And what is the purpose of causing such a fusion to occur? It is to reduce alienation, that feeling of not being quite a part of the world which is so characteristic of our time. This is the opposite of music as opiate, to which the surrealists objected. It is music to stimulate the creativity and critical capabilities of the audience.

If a member of the audience sees the score of the music, this member can ask himself legitimately, "What did this performer do? Where did he extend my vision of what that score could lead to? What did the performer fail to do which I, if I were able to perform, would like to have done? What did he do which I would like to see done even more?" Then, afterward, the member of the audience can ask, "What have I really seen happen? And what have I felt? What did it mean to me?" And when the member goes away, back to his or her private world at home, the same questions can continue to be asked.

But there is yet another aspect at work here; no audience is only a collection of its members. It also has a collective quality, as a community of participants, a community of people having a common experience. This is true of traditional music, of course, as well as of the kinds of music which I have been describing. The interesting thing here is that, if the horizons really fuse, so do the horizons of the members of the audience also fuse. Each member feels this as part of the experience, and the discussions after the concert show this—they are apt to be more creative and philosophical than after a traditional concert. The audience is stimulated rather than exhausted. This is not just another ideal: it is what *usually* happens when there is a really good concert of this sort, and it provides the music with its real *raison d'être,* which is not to write another clever symphony or sonata for the winning of prizes, but to share a vision of reality, to the end of, even if for only a moment, trying to reduce alienation and stimulating the best that is in the heads, the experience and the potentials of the members of the audience, both collectively and individually. We cannot, as composers, do that by blasting the audience into numbness; we can only do it by drawing them into the process of the work. The catharsis of Wagner's *Götterdämmerung* leads inexorably to Buchenwald. But there is a good chance that the new music, free of cathartic manipulations, leads to furthering the best capabilities of the community of men and women.

6 Underpiece/ Overpiece

If this were France or Germany, where the streets are paved with ideas instead of fools' gold, it would be easy to make up and publish a book on what we might call "underpiece" and "overpiece"—and to describe the book is my project for the moment. By "overpiece" what I mean is the work-beyond-the-work in any work of art, the idea of the work and the work stripped of any of its flaws in realization. By "underpiece" I mean the set of materials which constitute the realization of the work—its words, its sounds, its details and specifics, its components, its images, and all the aspects of its physical manifestation—its colors and its tastes, its characters and its forms. Speaking metaphorically, the "overpiece" is the *langue* or language of the work, while the "underpiece" is its *parole* or its word. In some cases the "overpiece" is greater or lesser than the sum of its *paroles,* but that we can come back to later. And in some cases the "overpiece" and the "underpiece" very nearly converge, which is a special case which would need a chapter in my book; but this too we can return to later.

Surely the book would need a section on each of the traditional genera of the arts—music, visual art, literature, dance, and, lately, the intermedia, and so on. But taken in brief the discussion could follow the lines of setting up a model or group of models or paradigms.

Taking music, for instance, one might consider some aspects of the Three C's of recent music—Cowell, Cage, and Corner. Cowell seemed very conscious of the overpiece/underpiece distinction. In the summer of 1959 I decided to walk from Woodstock, New York, all the way to the Canadian border—perhaps in emulation of a walk that Cowell had once made along, I believe, the whole of the West Coast of the USA. Alas, it was the wrong summer to do that. Every day I would hike up over Overlook Mountain and down to Shady, where Henry Cowell and his gracious wife

Sidney were staying in a friend's house while their own was being fixed up. And every day I meant to hike along past that, into the northern Catskills and beyond. But every day, when I came over the mountain, it would start to rain and storm, bitterly cold. So every day I would end up by arriving at the Cowells' house—where Henry and Sidney very patiently put up with my arrivals and questions, looked at whatever wild foods I had gathered or music I had been working on, and told marvelous stories—always to the point—and made useful comments on what I had brought. The fortnight during which this kept happening was one of the most rich experiences of my watershed year.

One day I was hiking down the mountain. The daily storm had passed and I was drenched and shivering (in spite of my poncho and two sweaters)—and as I went down the road I heard a perfectly dreadful caterwauling, as if a herd of pigs were being slaughtered. Slowly I came to realize that the sound was coming from where the Cowells were staying. I walked around the corner and there I found Henry with a dozen or so neighbors or musicians (apparently very amateur), and he had set them to performing some piece of his. The dissonance was quite extraordinary. But Henry was sitting quietly, listening to the "musicians" finish. The expression on his face was angelic and radiant. Clearly he was listening *through* the mistakes and dissonance of the "underpiece" of the moment in the overall experience and, without ignoring these, was perceiving and enjoying the hidden melodies and patterns. That is, of course, how many of Cowell's tone cluster pieces are to be taken—one must *perceive* what is going on as actively as a spectator at a boxing match, so that every element becomes transparent and the "overpiece" is revealed. Some of the tone cluster pieces conceal simple jigs inside them—or hymns. Others involve or include simple formal principles, much of whose beauty lies in their relation to the overpiece.

The process of active listening involves, then, a perception of the underpiece as transparent and a process of seeing through it to the overpiece. Once, in the summer of 1978, Malcolm Goldstein, the violinist and composer, came to see John Cage, who was visiting me. And with him he had the phonograph records of Ezra Pound's opera, *The Testament of Francois Villon,* which is very seldom performed. He put the phonograph records on my machine to share his experience with Cage. But after about two minutes, Cage asked him *please* to take the records off, he couldn't stand it.

What Cage was objecting to was the confusion between a recorded sound experience and an actual one, that the record sounded artificial (and, philosophically, *was* artificial) with its noises and distortions. Nor could any power on earth encourage him to see the recorded experience as a sort of *translation* from the original work, with its own set of "underpiece" *paroles* which were appropriate to it. He was so caught up by the underpiece that he could only see it as opaque and could not see through it to the overpiece.

This is strange because many of Cage's own works are transparent—one sees through their specificities, their various *paroles* or sounds and complexes of sounds, to the overpiece which is often a matter of conception, of philosophical idea and structure or of social vision. The work becomes a social paradigm, with each element treated democratically or autonomously, more or less independent from, or parallel to, each other. The materials are not forced to fit a Procrustean bed of form à la early Stockhausen, but behave independently; and the musicians are trusted, not told what they must do but, rather, allowed to realize their own unique capabilities. Each work has its overpiece which is its own *langue.* One senses the commonality of all possible realizations.

Corner very often composes in a way which follows this model also. He describes how the piece *is* when it is realized, rather than demanding that one *do* this and that. And if one performs such a piece, one simply lets it happen according to how its nature has been described as being, in terms of texture, characteristics, phenomenological change. If one superimposes one's taste or desire for personal expression over the piece, the underpiece of the realization will immediately become opaque and the overpiece will be hidden: so one plays midwife to the experience and helps it along into the world. When the piece opens its mouth, the performer must shut his. And the listener must be like Cowell—must listen through the underpiece to the overpiece, using his or her own life experiences and art experiences as means of penetrating through the underpiece. I recall an instance when Corner himself failed to do this; I was playing a 1960s piano piece of my own, *Emmett Williams's Ear,* which uses a graphic notation which I chose to interpret very dissonantly and with free rhythms. Corner pointed out, quite correctly, that the overall sound was very 1950s à la Boulez, and he seemed for that reason to be putting the piece down. But I pointed out to him that the piece was intended to be heard with the ears of the 1980s and beyond, that the 1950s element was merely the underpiece—it could, equally well, have been "realized" using Mozartian harmonies and phrases—while the more vital part of the work lay in its patternings and implications, which were far more contemporary. One should, then, see through the underpiece and accidents or specificities to the overpiece, not to the intention (the "intentional fallacy"—the assumption that one can know what the creator had in mind—leads to as many problems today as it did in the days of Ruskin or Pater) but to the essence. The pleasure of a musical experience lies in seeing the harmony between the overpiece and the underpiece, both of which are part of what the piece *is*, and both of which are equally necessary.

My book would have to have a section on literature, of course. And much of recent literature seems unsatisfactory for a reason that is hard to describe except by reference to this underpiece/overpiece distinction—it seems like so much *stuff,* with virtually no attention paid to the overpiece. This is particularly true of the work which has been influenced by Charles Olson. Olson's work looks Great, looks appropriate to the productions of a man who himself looked Great, all six feet five or six inches (or more?) of him. But Olson is at his best in poems like the

"Kingfishers," which is in essence a philosophical poem on the transcience of worldly things and cultures and cultural values. Yet Olson came out of the American pragmatic tradition which, by and large, rejected metaphysics and philosophy as being usable in the arts, which took William Carlos Williams's famous formulation, "No ideas but in things" to mean "No ideas" at least in the sense of being separable from the underpiece. The result is that the text is made deliberately opaque; there seems to be no overpiece at all. It is almost as if one were making a poetic parallel to the political orator to whom Calvin Coolidge, the former American president, listened patiently for some hours; Coolidge went home to his wife, who asked what the orator had spoken about. Said Coolidge, "He didn't say." It is not that one need demand that all literary works be forced to be *about* something; after all, narrative or ratiocination is only one possible way to organize material. But is, for example, one made up a set of words, and one then set it into alphabetical order, this revelation of the process or experience of alphabeticalization would constitute an overpiece, or at least a formal element which implied some kind of overpiece, and a really perceptive listener would then hear through the words to that overpiece (or read through them).

My book would have to have sections on performance and on the visual arts and certainly would have to take into account "conceptual art," most of which is inadequate for the opposite reason of the problem with Olsonite poetry: very often it seems all at the service of the overpiece, with insufficient fleshing out into an underpiece to reveal all aspects of the overpiece. A very simple overpiece, for example, can be adequately realized by matching it up with a minimal underpiece which fully implies it. An instance of this would be the minimalist artist George Brecht's work which consists of the word "green" in raised letters on a flat surface, and the whole work colored, overall—red. But many conceptual and minimalist pieces seem to use very complex overpieces—metaphysical principles, personal histories—which the underpiece can only inadequately reveal. The result seems to be a mismatch which the perceiver of the work feels as too cerebral. The matching of overpiece and underpiece is extraordinarily complex in minimalist works, and even the spectator must be extraordinarily perceptive if he or she is to perceive the suitability of a given match; this perception is an acquired skill, of course, but then it always was—only the best of critics can appreciate the suitability of a particular subject to a fugue, or an arrangement of figures in space to a particularly fine painting by Poussin. But, if the spectator is as hedonistic as he or she is perceptive, pleasure will be a part of the experience. For every work is an example of *something,* and that something is an indicator of context. The perceiver (or spectator or listener) who can fully experience the context of a work can see the overpiece far more readily than a person to whom the context is unclear, and is thus baffling.

Thus, particularly in these new kinds of work, where the overpiece is critical, philosophical works where one gets not the ratiocination of a philosophy but its feeling, the spectator must not just make a simple taxonomy of the piece, as if he or she were a passive listener to an entertaining piece of old-time popular music, but must understand that he or she is understanding it in order to understand it at all. Stressing that process of understanding reflexively, asking oneself "What is it to like what I am liking? What is it to understand what I am understanding?"—this process belongs to the branch of philosophy which Gadamer and the post-Heideggerian philosophers call "hermeneutics," and the most useful sort of criticism which we could now create and that would allow us to share our favorable experiences of the new arts would be a hermeneutic criticism. Surely it would be far more rewarding than, for instance, the currently fashionable new criticism that is based on purely linguistic principles—structuralism which is dear to the academics, but which often amounts to far-out ways of looking at Balzac, or Derridean poststructuralism in which the critical terms reveal nothing but themselves and which is, in any case, so verbocentric as to be useless for music, visual art, performance art, or, ultimately, poetry. Ah well, my book would probably have to have a long chapter on hermeneutics as opposed to these other approaches, and perhaps adding to hermeneutics some elements of semiotics, which is the study of how things mean what they do; for the meaning of a work of concept art or of a Cagean piece of music or of such new poems as myself or Jackson Mac Low often write—such meaning is often emblemmatic, intrinsically meaningless (which sounds paradoxical), but which acquires its meaning from its cultural context, from the ability of the listener or spectator or other perceiver to assign a suitable context to the overpiece.

Overpiece and underpiece—I hope someone writes my book some day. It would be exciting to read.

7 Postmodern Performance: Some Criteria and Common Points

The Moment that one tries to treat those ideas which are associated with the term "postmodern" concretely, and specifically to apply them to the performance arts, issues and questions are raised which were not anticipated. Even at best "postmodern" is a curious near-oxymoron, covering some forty years of cultural history in which the performance arts, I think it could be argued, have changed even more than the others, so that while the academics speak of Samuel Beckett as "postmodern" their students think of him as a neo-romantic. During the "postmodern" period, myths have become objectivized and are usually treated very electically simultaneity has become characteristic of communications, forms have become more interpenetrative with their subjects than they had been, many themes have ceased to be presented with logi (either emotional or rational) and are instead presented intuitively as allusions, and narrative, if any, lost its primacy and became either simply scenario or disappeared altogether except for ornament. In the first part of the postmodern period we have the works which begin this evolution—the works of Beckett and Genet, of the theater, of the absurd, of abstract expressionist and *tachiste* painting (the early work of The Living Theater or more recent work by Claus Bremer would be examples of the principles of these being applied to the theater), and to such trends in American poetry as the Black Mountain School of Charles Olson and his followers, or of the New York intuitive styles of John Ashbery or Kenneth Koch.

But sometime around 1958 a second major shift began to crystallize which I have elsewhere called "postcognitivism"—which actually means "postself-cognitivism. Here the overt message follows the narrative into the near-limbo of being mere ornament, the artist ceases to create his own myth (as he had been doing, typically, since the mid-nineteenth century), and the areas of sensual experience or discipline came to be less discrete than they had been. At times these tended to fuse into the *intermedia*—concrete poetry, for example, which fuses text and visual art, sound poetry which fuses text and music conceptually and does not simply mix them, or the happening, which is a three-way intermedium or fusion of text/drama, visual art, and music, or the "event" which is the minimalist analogue of the happening—as in fluxus works. All the arts were affected by this shift; the novel, for instance, became almost out of sequence from its immediate ancestry once visual elements and nonsyntactic prose began to be really common in the works, as in, say, Federman in America, Kutter in Switzerland, Roche in France, etc. The principles of chance or aleatoric structures ceased to be the property of a single school and became stock in trade for poets of many groups, for composers such as Pousseur or Kagel, artists like George Brecht of fluxus, and so on. The ferment which all this fusion produced made the 1960s even more innovative than the 1920s had been—the most innovative decade in recent Western cultural history, in fact.

The critics lagged behind. They saw each fusion of sensibility not as a process but as a separate and definitive trend or movement, thus creating the illusion of a concrete poetry movement, a pop art movement, a happenings movement, a fluxus movement, and so on. The resulting conceptual confusion drove many of them into a formalistic Marxism which, in its own terms at least, explained a lot but dealt with the issues raised by these new art fusions only obliquely and inadequately. There was little or no connection between the formal Marxism of the *Art and Language* group of critics, for instance, and the more intuitive Marxism of many of the artists whose impetus in doing these new arts came from an attempt to do artwork which was more appropriate to the real needs, real people, and real intellectual currents of the time, of the historical moment.

In many cases the critics retreated into theory that had little or no relevance to practice, at least no relevance to the practice of the only time they knew at firsthand—the art of the present. Structuralism was centered in academia and in Paris which, for the most of this period, was the

Postmodern
Performance
72

most conservative of major cities—even the most conservative city, artistically, in France where recent innovations have come more often from Bordeaux, Limoges, or Nice than from Paris. Thus structuralism tended to become a matter of far-out ways of looking at Balzac than what it might have, a set of criteria for understanding one's immediate experience of the new arts. This led to strange things such as the praise of Maurice Roche, a sort of Frenchified offshoot of Emilio Villa, at the expense of real innovators such as Robert Filliou; the theory of structuralism and poststructuralism was very interesting, but its implications for artistic innovation were for the most part ignored. Similarly, hermeneutics remained, for the most part, the domain of professors or university philosophers, the province of specialists. Its applicability to the problems of graphic notation in music, for instance, were not explored—and, in fact, *have* not been until now, relevant though they are to some of the music of John Cage, Philip Corner, Charlie Morrow, Pauline Oliveros, etc.

Through this last twenty years or so, the United States, which experienced a very productive time in its creative arts, was a backwash for criticism and theory—its critics knew much more about getting grant applications in or qualifying to get tenture at universities than they did about the new arts. The United States became a critical backwash, haunted by the ghosts of the New Critics and by the myth of American originality. This last myth, originally cultivated as a defense for our growing independence from Europe, came to be a sort of ideology of the ostrich: "We don't want to see how good your European art is, so we won't." The writing in art journals such as the *Fox* (ultraleftist), *Artforum* (Fabian and paternalist), or *Art and Letters* (ultraelitist) seemed curiously out of phase with the best work that was coming from France, Germany, Italy, Scandinavia, or Japan. It was as technical as these, but it was a technicalized and jargon-ridden academicized overlay on ideas whose relevance was to the world of half a century before, and which could not be *lived* as vital criticism is lived, as part of the commonality of understanding one's newest cultural experience.

This brings us to the vacuum of the mid- and late-1970s. Happenings are passé, we are told: it says so in the media. But the media have been saying that since happenings began. Thus, since the impetus which created happenings in the first place still exists, when young artists "do a-what comes natchurly" and come up with happenings, they must be represented under the new name—"art performances." It is true they have a different style, typically, from the old happenings—there is no longer abstract expressionism to react against, the great protests against America's involvement in the Vietnam fiasco are gone with the passions that they aroused, the pop art urbanism is gone and there is a new emphasis on a holistic social view which includes the problems and potentials of the countryside and agriculture. The taste is for "cooler" things now—"cool" in McLuhan's sense—objective and detached. A new positivism is afoot. The imperative seems to be: "be satisfied to work with things and to mistrust principles." The arts seem cleaner than they did—less interpenetrative with ideas. For instance, the young performance artist—could we call him a happenings artist?—Stuart Sherman makes up a sort of theater of small objects. He spreads things out on a large table, sorts them, and moves with them, demonstrates conventional and unconventional ways of using them. But the criticism—both method and specific analysis—which would be *appropriate* to such performances has not emerged. Perhaps what we need is an *appropriate* criticism, something to parallel *appropriate* technology (which is the new watchword in that area). We need a hermeneutics that is not just for specialists, a structuralism which relates to the language of things and not to the fashions in French departments, a poststructuralism which uses the ideas of Derrida or every Lyotard positively in order to explain what one *feels* when one hears a chant by Charlie Morrow rather than merely to attack what a few French professors said twenty years ago. In short, we need a repository of sets of critical approaches and ideas from which we can develop this appropriate criticism. The devil in our universities is not their intellectualism but their politics, their trendiness; thus it is hard to say whether it is possible for such a criticism to come from or to center on our universities. Only to the extent to which a university is free to be an intellectual center is it possible.

Rather, then, than starting from criticism and developing ideas about what one will or will not experience *in vacuo* (so far as artistic practice is concerned)—which means that real dialectic is between what one says and the rules and practices of university politics—why not start from some of the ideas common in very recent performance arts, and generalize from them?

One idea is that each work has a unique gestalt which no single performance or notation can totally realize. The term is used widely these days, by performance artists as different as Newton and Helen Harrison, Philip Corner, Alison Knowles, and the dancer Meredith Monk. The character or persona *in* a work, the thematic concept, and abstract values, each are subordinate to this gestalt and must be so thoroughly embedded in it that they do not overwhelm it lest they wreck its texture. Thus the role of "idea" becomes different from what it was in pre-postcognitive art, literature, or discourse: one can evoke an idea, but one is not to prove or to demonstrate it. This is true both of abstract principle and of characterization. Thus, in Meredith Monk's *Songs from the Hill,* sound poems, actually each of the "songs" evokes a psychological mask or persona in the way a ballet dancer does in character dancing. After each song the character returns to the limbo from which it emerged. In Alison Knowles' *Bean Garden* she performed with her (my) twelve-year-old daughter: a gestalt appeared of mother and child, part of another gestalt of dailiness. The gestalt of the work is, then, part of a linkage of other gestalts, neither subordinate nor superior to it. The gestalt is a quality which the work realizes based on its materials; it is what it exemplifies. But it is not, for example, a hypothesis or a message in the sense of being a separable idea, capable of proof or demonstration.

The second point of concensus has to do with the self-image of the artist: the traditional self-image projected by an artist is a consistent one, while the postcognitive one is often nearly obliterated or anonymized besides. When a traditional composer such as Charles Ives took a sound experience from his personal experience, he turned it into Ivesiana. But the postcognitive artist tends to leave it be, for the most part unchanged. Thus instead of creating a mythic personality for himself or herself, the postcognitive artist tends to make the working materials assume mythic or archetypal characteristics. Alison Knowles working with her daughter becomes Everywoman working with hers. Where in earlier postmodern modes—what I can only call with a horrendous neologism, "pre-postcognitive"—a Charles Olson would not write the poem that needed writing but would imitate the kind of poem that his self-mythic Olson would produce and would thus create a dialogue between the poet and his poethood, the postcognitive artist creates more a dialogue between working material and its myths, between lightbulb and the idea of a lightbulb.

Thus, in postcognitive thinking, the focus lies on the work and not the worker. The impetus to be consistent—in the sense that one might imagine Charles Olson felt the need to do things according to his public and professional image—is not felt in the area of expression, but only of ongoing concern. The new artist says: "I am interested in beans, so I will use them until such a time as I am no longer interested in beans." Thus the postcognitive artist no longer creates a fully formed persona of himself or herself, but creates only the momentary and tentative gestalt, subject to change and modification. If he or she sees that thus and such needs doing, then he or she does it. No matter that *A* is a so-called painter, if she feels that some poem needs making, she makes it. This is inherent in the psychology of what Richard Kostelanetz calls "polyartists." In the past artists expanded their horizons in order to extend the challenges within a recognized categorical channel—to try themselves in new worlds. Today they simply follow their natural interests, their intuitive curiosity, their wondering whether this or that would "work." The avoidance of expression is not some form of hebephrenia—the pathological condition in which there is a phobia of emotion—but an unwillingness to impose oneself needlessly on the materials with which one is working. Where traditionally the expression was used to create the artist's persona—Beethoven as the mad and passionate genius, for instance—the gestalt of the artist today is directed only onto the mythic level. One thinks of Charlotte Moorman, for instance, as *"the* topless cellist" (mythic) more than as an individual woman artist from Little Rock, Arkansas (actual).

Here there arises the crucial distinction between *acting,* in the old art, and *enacting* in the new art. Edmund Kean *acted* King Lear; today we *enact* our rituals of performance, stressing the materials of performance more than our own identities. You do not come to a John Cage concert to hear the Great Fuggitutti perform the Master's Immortal Masterpiece. You come to hear certain sounds which will be meaningful to you, to see and hear certain things which will enrich your cultural or aesthetic experience. Skills may be involved; they usually are. Paul Zukowsky, who plays Cage's recent violin pieces, is a consummately skillful violinist. But he has better things to do than to act out the role of the Great Paul—which would detract from the significance and stature of his performing. If Cage happens to be present and performing, he does not do so *de rostro* as a great man or great authority but as an active and involved participant. Or, in performing in a happening or a fluxus event, one performer is more or less replaceable by another so long as there exist the physical capability of doing a given performance task and the spiritual appropriateness of that task to be done by the performer at hand. Character is relative, not absolute. One *is* what one *does,* and style proceeds from the gestalt of a particular work. It would seem tyrannic to require that the same style be used for subsequent works for the sake of consistency to one's so-called identity, especially if those works are made for quite different situations, locations, and purposes. Perhaps one can assert, though this is hard to demonstrate, that in place of an artist's consistent and ongoing persona or ego, that the ego is replaced by a superego, an objectified, generalized, and mythicized version of the artist, used as both a poetic reference and as a genius implied by the work. The "artist" becomes a metaphor, while the particular artist remains hard at work.

Turning to another area, the intermedia are necessarily synchretic. That is, they fuse elements from various wholes rather than allowing each element to remain simultaneously present, distinguishable, discrete, and potentially capable of being separated out of the work. The newer performance artists, conscious of the implications of their intermedia, seem to take a synchretic approach to their cultural contexts as well. That is, not only do they tend to fuse visual art, heard art, spoken art, and poetry, but they often fuse in elements from other cultures and civilizations, which are borrowed not for any exoticism (exoticism, after all, is ephemeral and vanishes with familiarity—South America is only exotic to people who have not lived or been there), but for their appropriateness to the work at hand. Often they tend to swell the context with which the new artist works. For instance, there are the event pieces which are very similar to fluxus works, which Jerome Rothenberg culled from South Pacific cultures in his *Rituals* and *Technicians of the Sacred* books. There is no need to be authentic in such pieces. The older question in performance, central to existentialism or to the Stanislavskian method, may have been: "Who am I being when I am being someone else?" Often the unspoken question of new performance works seems to be, "Has anyone besides us made performances like ours? Are there precedents for them, or are they unique to our here and now?" The significance of this kind of synchretism of cultures seems to be its answer to that question: "No matter how different these new works may be from traditional western performance art forms, they have precedents in the human experience outside the west," and this context helps to give them legitimacy by establishing itself as a referent that is far more broadly based than some urban, Western-world avant-garde alone.

I am what I can do. This is one of our ruling maxims in the new arts. Charlie Morrow chants—and syncretizes elements from the Siouxan, Hebrew, and oriental traditions into one whole. He also writes (and composes) television jingles for a living. When he chants, is he a jingle writer chanting? When he writes jingles, is he a chanter writing jingles? An older generation would have answered yes to both questions. But for postmodern performance artists—especially recent, postcognitive ones, there is not so much a question of having a multiple identity as a polyvalent one. One extends one's artistic and personal identity by doing a variety of things. Sometimes it even seems to be assumed that a greater identity—in the sense of a broader capability and scope—is qualitatively "better" than a lesser one. This is, I think, very debatable; but it is an idea that is encountered very often. Each performance artist seems to feel that he or she should have worked in videotape and cinema as well as live performance. A festival of sound poetry is announced and—lo and behold!—all kinds of poets and artists produce their first sound poems—some quite good ones. Strange, how they seem to feel that their message is incomplete without such polymathic catholicity. And so it is with the individual performer in the individual work. Meredith Monk has remarked in a lecture about the difficulty she had, in teaching a choreographic work of hers, in getting any one of a group of new performers to do the variety of things which Lannie Harrison, a member of her original group, "The House," had done in its first production, and how she had to break up the part and divide it among several performers. However, note that she did so. The emphasis was on the things that were to be done. Can one imagine how in a similar situation, a choreographer might arrange to have a pas de deux in *Swan Lake* danced by three dancers, on the ground that no pairs of them could do what the choreographer had in mind? Here then is yet another characteristic of many new works: the number of performers is open, but the things that are to be done are fixed. Monk spoke of a new work then in progress as being either a vocal quartet or a full-fledged theater work. Knowles and Corner specify what they want to happen but say only that it is to be realized by from one to five performers. This can be working "at degree zero" in Roland Barthes's sense without its being anything which an orthodox structuralist could explain. But what this approach uniquely enables is the taking advantage of a particular performer's capabilities, on the one hand, and the consistent inclusion of some intention or intended body of material on the other. John Cage has fixed four particular singers as his instruments for one recent orchestral work. When one or more cannot be present, rather than make a substitution, he uses a tape of a performance by that performer. This complements Meredith Monk's division of materials among new performers, but it is not its opposite. Rather it is just an alternative way of guaranteeing that such and such a piece will *always* include such and such material, quite independently of the vagaries of traditional performance style. The work is the process of its realization, and is not some fixed ideal toward which any given realization merely aspires. There can be no definitive performance here, as there might with a symphonic work of Mozart, Berlioz or Schoenberg. One gets, instead, samplings may be brilliant, but there is always the consciousness that one is experiencing only one of several ways in which a given work could be realized.

Of course there has always been *some* sense of the change of meaning of a work, the shift in how an audience has experienced this or that work through its history. But in the recent works I have mentioned, the audience is encouraged to be active-minded rather than passive, and not only to see the work as it is taking place but to project, imaginatively, alternates as well. If it is clear that a work moves from point A to point B, then one thing a spectator must do is imagine A and B and C as well, in order to see why a work is as it is and to appreciate any unique character or strength in a given realization. One sees through the work to its gestalts. One sees through the performance to the gestalt of the work. Thus there is in all such postcognitive performance art an activity of watching the process on a plurality of levels. One cannot sit back, like the old ladies of Boston at a Tchaikovsky concert, with eyes closed and breasts heaving, waiting to be ravished emotionally. Rather one must be like the witness at a ritual or a crime, or like the public at a boxing match, being both in tune emphatically with what one is seeing and mentally dealing with the tactics of each move. One will be lost if one looks for passive thrills. As one performance artist remarked, Geoffrey Hendricks it was, "Ya won't get 'em." But if one lets the mind wander, if one queries what one sees, if one feels it in relation to what one already knows or has felt, then the experience of "watching the process" is a very rich one, deeply satisfying, uniquely so. Taking art as process, then, makes new and interesting experiences possible, which is ultimately the best justification for an innovation in art.

8 Performance, Taken Socially

A large part of what we see artists doing when they do work is doing things for their own sake, for what is intrinsically interesting in it and for the sharing of their experience. It is then incumbent upon us, who comprise the audience, to establish a dialectic between what the artist seems, to us, to be doing and what we choose, if anything, to contribute to that process to the ends of our own enrichment and of reexperiencing our own identities in relationship to what the artist is doing and in relationship to our own surrounding and daily worlds. To this dialectic we bring our own prejudgments, not in the sense of the usually negative "prejudice," but inevitably as part of our own previous experience which we use to get us "into" the work which we are experiencing. We are told that such-and-such a performance will be a musical concert, let us say, at which there will be a Beethoven piano concerto. We do not, therefore, worry too much about the choreography of the performance; our prejudgments are not those we would employ if we were going to watch a dance by George Ballanchine or Meredith Monk. Perhaps we do not like Beethoven very much; even so, we are at the concert, and for the sake of our own pleasure, we had better decide that we are going to use all our previous experience of classical music in order to participate, actively, as witnesses of the Beethoven concerto. To do otherwise would make for a very unpleasant musical experience and afternoon or evening.

Thus there is an important taxonomic element, even before we begin to watch a performance take place, a prejudgment according to past experience, which will condition what are the grounds from which we will adsorb the artistic work. Fluxus pieces are among those which investigated the limits and problems of this aspect of performance; it would have been very fluxus to label an evening "Renaissance Instrumental Music" and then to perform only open-ended "event" performance pieces. However, in time, even the word *fluxus* when it was associated with a concert tended to suggest the suspension of this element of prejudgment, so that it brought about new prejudgments on the part of the potential audience.

What this means is that, for the audience, the labeling of a performance work is part of the performance; it tells us something taxonomically, in terms of the kind of work which we will see, and also something our association with the performers' names connotes. Few of us would go to see "an inexplicable performance by red-haired cross-eyed male musicians," tempting though this might be for a moment—we would probably set such an evening low on our priorities of time. But we might go see "Dublin Ballads" sung by the fictitious O'Rourke Brothers (who might happen to have red hair and crossed eyes). So it is even with fluxus; of late the name has been debased by Ben Vautier's cabarets and insistence on performing only *old* fluxus pieces—so a new name is needed and, presto, the audience is excited. "Art performance" became a catchall in the late 1970s, so now, in the 1980s, we get "free-form performances." And we go.

Of course the new artists in every decade like to insist upon their own uniqueness—and with regard to the details of what they are doing, they are probably quite correct. But no human endeavor is without roots—the only way to be *wholly* original is to be wholly irrelevant. This or that generation may suppress some natural line of inquiry—for example, the Aristotelian poets from the 1660s to the 1950s suppressed the impulse to combine visual art and poetry; but when the Aristotelian current became tired (with its insistence that art must *move* its viewers, readers, listeners, or spectators), the visual impulse reappeared and we got "concrete poetry," seemingly new but actually an old and perfectly valid possibility, as it had been all along. Similarly, in the late 1950s when happenings and events appeared, they seemed more novel than they were—actually aesthetic rituals and events had been with us all along, in summer camps and among "primitive" tribes (as Jerome Rothenberg's *Technicians of the Sacred,* an anthology of rites and events from "primitive cultures," but which juxtaposes them with thenew events of the 1960s, makes clear). In the 1970s a new element was added to this particular mix—narratives, which had been rare in happenings and fluxus. At the time this seemed like a radical break with work of the 1960s (I am thinking of works by Michael Smith, Ralston Farina, and others), but from the present viewpoint the break seems far less radical, far less dramatic. The artist verbalizes his or her uniqueness and is therefore, and to that extent, not a very reliable source for our critical framing processes; we need continuities as well as discontinuities, and few artists can provide these.

But our criticism has tended to focus too much on the artist, to little on the work, for which the starting point is the spectator. We need a hermeneutics of the audience, in order for the audience to become enthusiastic about the results of the artist's endeavors—and for that we do not yet have even the beginnings of a common vocabulary. If there is any grounds for the feeling of isolation on the part of the artist, it lies here; it is not that the work itself is so difficult—those who get used to the new works find them delightful, but often they are unable to explain why. So, in the meantime, our learned teachers babble on in their neo-Aristotelian way, our political brethren say that such-and-such work is inherently unpopular, our journalists sell newspapers in the same old way, and the achievements of our performing artists go along misunderstood; really, there is no reason why this should be—it's a matter of generating what is technically a hermeneutic of the audience, and in due course, no doubt it will appear. But for this to happen, as I said at the outset, our attention must be focused not on the dancer but on the dance, not on the personality of the woman who gives a performance in which she uses only information on beans, but on the beans themselves and on the relationship to beans of each and every member of the audience (I am thinking of Alison Knowles now). We are not only the witnesses of such a performance but are also the co-creators of it.

And what is the art which is least realistic? It is, any artwork in which the reality of the work is beside the point, artwork which accepts its own forms by rote—telling a story in an automatic way, providing material for the musicians to perform as automatons, filling out anthologies of "new art performances" because the artist wants to get his or her name into print, hanging on the walls of art galleries because it's professionally desirable for the artist to do so. Such art can be clever, but it can never be fully satisfying—having a career for its own sake is the one sake that leads inexorably to dead ends. Similarly, the best way to evaluate the works which one sees, all of them unfamiliar we will assume, in a show or on a dance program is to ask oneself, "Would this work exist if it were not for this show/concert/institution where I am experiencing it?" If not—then forget it. But if one has a sense that there is an intrinsic involvement between the artist and his or her materials—then trust the artist and proceed to the next phases of asking what is it, and why is it as it is. A real career is not what is listed in an artist's resumé—it is rather the trajectory of satisfied involvements, both for the artist and for the spectator; in this sense Beethoven is neither the man nor the list of his works but is the complex of our experience of those works in our own lives. And the avant-garde, be it ever so unfamiliar, is not different from this. Thus it is we who make the new arts, not just the artists—we, as members of society experiencing those cultural artifacts which are offered to us, on the basis of their intrinsic interest for us. A journalist can tell us that "so-and-so" is big in Paris/New York/Milano/Toronto, but we will not return for more such works unless we have found intrinsic interest. The artist's career is of no interest to us, for all its possible glamor, if the work lacks this intrinsicality of interest; and thus it is for the intrinsic elements that we must look.

I see a performance by an unknown dancer; I empathize with her moves. The form puzzles and challenges me. I sense that she is doing as she is doing because she must. I look for the source of that compulsion; I discover in it a new language of movement? I learn to understand that language if not to speak it, and I am enriched. I will return for more. The name on the program is no longer merely the name of the woman; it is now the name of a part of that language, a point in a new trajectory of satisfactions. The critics can affect my prejudgments, but they cannot affect my experience. This dancer has given me a transfer from her mind to mine—an example of something in her language. (Once I wrote *An Exemplativist Manifesto* on this part of the process.) I accept it; perhaps what I find meaningful is not what she intended, but that is not the point. More important is that this language itself has enriched me. Her horizon has met mine, and the two have fused at some points. That suffices.

9 A Child's History of Fluxus

Long long ago, back when the world was young—that is, sometime around the year 1958—a lot of artists and composers and other people who wanted to do beautiful things began to look at the world around them in a new way (for them).

They said: "Hey!—coffee cups can be more beautiful than fancy sculptures. A kill in the morning can be more dramatic than a drama by Mr. Fancypants. The sloshing of my foot in my wet boot sounds more beautiful than fancy organ music."

And when they saw that, it turned their minds on. And they began to ask questions. One question was: "Why does everything I see that's beautiful like cups and kisses and sloshing feet have to be made into just a part of something fancier and bigger? Why can't I just use it for its own sake?"

When they asked questions like that, they were inventing fluxus; but *this* they didn't know yet, because fluxus was like a baby whose mother and father couldn't agree on what to call it—they knew it was there, but it didn't have a name.

Well, these people were scattered all over the world. In America there were George (George Brecht) and Dick (Dick Higgins) and LaMonte (LaMonte Young) and Jackson (Jackson Mac Low) and plenty of others. In Germany there were Wolf (Wolf Vostell) and Ben and Emmett (Ben Patterson and Emmett Williams) who were visiting there from America, and there was another visitor in Germany too from a very little country on the other side of the world, from Korea—his name was Nam June Paik. Oh there were more too, there and in other countries also.

They did "concerts" of everyday living; and they gave exhibitions of what they found, where they shared the things that they liked best with whoever would come. Everything was itself, it wasn't part of something bigger and fancier. And the fancy people didn't like this, because it was all cheap and simple, and nobody could make much money out of it.

But these people were scattered all over the world. They sometimes knew about each other, but they didn't see each other much or often. And they spoke different languages and had different names for what they were doing, even when they were doing the same thing. It was all mixed up.

Well, LaMonte had a pal—another George, George Maciunas: his name looked strange but sounded easy enough—"Ma-choó-nuss." And George Maciunas liked to make books. So LaMonte said, "Let's do a book of our kind of thing." And his friend Jackson agreed. And they did it. LaMonte collected the things for the book, and George Maciunas put it onto pages, and after a while, they were able to take it to a printer and have it printed. They called the book "An Anthology" which is a fun word for a collection. No fancy name. Not "A Fluxus Anthology," because fluxus things weren't named yet. Just "An Anthology." It was a beautiful book and you can still buy it and look at the beautiful, simple things in it*—ideas and piles of words and ways for making your own life more wonderful.

Well, it costs money to make books, and if you spend your money on one thing you can't spend it on another. George Maciunas had rented a beautiful big room in the fanciest part of New York City, and there he had an art gallery where fluxus kinds of things were shown and shared or allowed to happen. But when there was no money to pay for all that, once the book was done, George Maciunas had to give up his AG Gallery, as he called it; and he decided to go to Germany. With him he took some big boxes all chockablock full of leftover things that LaMonte and the others had collected, but which didn't fit into the "Anthology."

George Maciunas's idea was to get together with the people in Germany who were doing the same kind of thing, and to do something like a book and something like a magazine—it would be printed every so often, and it would always change, always

---

*LaMonte Young, ed. *An Anthology*, 1970. (Available from: DIA Art Foundation, 112 Franklin Street, New York, N.Y. 10013.)

be different, always be really itself. It needed a name. So George Maciunas chose a very funny word for "change"—fluxus. And he started taking fluxus things to the printers in Germany, to make his magazine. To let people know about this kind of book, he decided to give some fluxus concerts there, so the newspapers would write about them and people would find out about his books.

So in September 1962 the first of the fluxus concerts happened in a little city where George Maciunas was living, in Wiesbaden, Germany (you say that—"Vees'-bodd-en"). Dick went there from New York, with Alison (Alison Knowles) his artist wife, and they took with them lots of pieces by other American people who had been finding and sharing fluxus kinds of things.

The concerts certainly did get written about! They were on television too. Poor George Maciunas's mother! She was an old-fashioned lady, and when the television showed all the crazy things that her son George was doing at the fluxus concerts, she was so embarrassed that she wouldn't go out of her house for two weeks because she was so ashamed of what the neighbors might say. Oh well, you have to expect that kind of thing. Actually some of the neighbors really liked the fluxus concerts. The janitor at the museum where the fluxus concerts were happening liked them so well that he came to every performance with his wife and children.

By and by other museums and public places wanted fluxus concerts too. So fluxus concerts happened next in England and Denmark and France. And new pieces kept being found or done—fluxus people (we called them "fluxpeople") sent things from Japan and Holland and all kinds of places. Fluxus got famous.

And then fluxus began to get copied. Fancy people began copying fluxus things and ideas. But they tried to make fancy things out of them—and that changed them. When teacups were replaced by millions of teacups they weren't simple any more, so they stopped being fluxus. That was always the difference: they stopped being part of life. You could always tell the real fluxus things from the fake ones because the real ones stayed simple, while the fake ones had fancy names attached to them.

Once fame began to happen George Maciunas and the other fluxus people had to figure out what to do next to keep fluxus fun and working for everybody. George liked to be the boss; but he was smart enough to know that he couldn't be boss and tell the fluxus artist what to do, because they'd quit and they were mostly better artists than he was. So he became the chairman instead. That meant that he couldn't tell people what they *had* to do, or what they must *not* do if they wanted to stay part of fluxus; instead he could tell the world what fluxus *was*, and anyone who wanted to do that kind of thing was Fluxus. That was smart because it meant the fluxus people didn't break up into gangs that disagreed, the way lots of artists' groups did before that. They stuck together to do fluxus kinds of things, even when they were also doing other kinds of things at the same time.

Twice George Maciunas forgot this. Once, in the winter of 1963, Dick and Alison went to Sweden and gave fluxus concerts; but there was no money to buy tickets so George Maciunas or Ben or Emmett could come to Sweden. So Dick (that's me) and Alison gave the concerts with new Swedish fluxus people there. George got very angry and told Dick and Alison they couldn't be fluxus people any more. But so what: nobody paid any attention to that, because Dick and Alison were doing fluxus concerts of things by Ben and Emmett and George (Brecht) and Bob (Watts) and the Japanese fluxus people and so on. It was fun and it was fluxus, which was what counted.

In 1963 George Maciunas came back to America. He opened a fluxus store and gave fluxus festivals. The German fluxus people came to visit; so did the artists' groups did before that. They stuck together to do fluxus kinds of French ones. Invitations began to come from fancy places—museums and colleges; but the fluxus people were too smart to get involved with those. They would have lost their freedom. So the colleges and museums got the fake fluxus people and things (and they still have them, *mostly*). You could tell the fakes because they weren't themselves: because of their famous names. The real things were much cheaper, and this confused the fancy folk. But oh well.

But by 1965 some of the fluxus people themselves began to get famous. This would have been okay, except that George Maciunas didn't know how to handle them anymore. He kept trying to be boss. He got very very angry when a group of fluxus people decided to join some artists who weren't fluxus people in a big performance that was kind of a circus, called *Originale* ("Or-ee-ghee-noll-eh"). Maciunas and his friend Henry Flynt tried to get the fluxus people to march around outside the circus with white cards that said *Originale* was bad. And they tried to say that the fluxus people who were in the circus weren't fluxus any more. That was silly, because it made a split. I thought it was funny, and so first I walked around with Maciunas and with Henry with a card, then I went inside and joined the circus; so both groups got angry with me. Oh well. Some people say that fluxus died that day—I once thought so myself—but it turned out I was wrong.

Why was I wrong? Because Fluxus things still needed doing and fluxus people kept on doing them. Maciunas kept printing fluxus things—cards and games and ideas—and putting them into little plastic boxes that were more fun than most books. I made little books that were really fluxus, though they didn't have that name on them. And every so often there were fluxconcerts.

And there still are.

A lot of time has gone by now. As I write this it is almost 1980. George Maciunas died last year of a long and horrible illness. But he knew before he died that his mistake was forgiven, that all the fluxus people were together again—they came together for concerts, for New Years' parties, for many things like that. And when Maciunas was dying, they came together to his house to help him finish up a lot of his fluxus boxes and works before he died. When Maciunas went into the hospital for the last time, his doctors said, "We don't know why this man is still alive." But the fluxus people knew. Being friends and sharing simple things can be so very important.

And though fluxus is almost twenty years old now—or maybe more than twenty, depending on when you want to say it began—there are still new fluxus people coming along, joining the group. Why? Because fluxus has a life of its own, apart from the old people in it. It is simple things, taking things for themselves and not just as part of bigger things. It is something that many of us must do, at least part of the time. So fluxus is inside you, is part of how you are. It isn't just a bunch of things and dramas but is part of how you live. It is beyond words.

When you grow up, do you want to be part of fluxus? I do.

10 Some Thoughts on the Context of Fluxus

Here we are in 1978, some sixteen years after the first formal manifestations of fluxus and nearly twenty years after the first groupings together of the international artists who later congealed into fluxus. A few have died: Richard Maxfield and Arthur Køpcke. A few have disappeared. A few have retreated into academia and conservative art. And yet the splits which ended (prematurely?) the earlier syncretic and iconoclastic art movements of this century—futurism, dadaism, surrealism, perhaps more—simply have not occurred. We still work together on occasion—there is no money in our fluxwork, so we do other work as well, in or out of art. But how can it be that this strangely diverse group of artists from disparate origins and disparate ages, who seem unbound by a coherent ideology, stay together?

The first reason lies, I think, in the nature of the lineage of which fluxus is a part. Here I can only speak of Western culture, since our Eastern, Japanese branch, has obviously different roots, though I would be amazed if there were not cultural parallels. One key assumption of fluxus works is that there are close analogies among things—that the linguistic of shoes and of horses can have certain points in common, enough to establish a conceptual pattern, and that for this reason an aesthetically satisfying realization can be made of an aesthetic concept using either shoes or horses as the instrumentation. Projected onto the aesthetics of art (and of course not all aesthetics are the aesthetics of art) and viewed from this perspective, the behavior of the different arts (including the art of thought, philosophy) is sufficiently close that these are properly seen as media, with the ground between such media, then, the *inter*-media—and each intermedium can become, in its own right, a new medium as it becomes more established as a point of reference. Thus, concrete poetry and calligraphy are both intermedia between literature and the visual arts, but there could also be an intermedium between concrete poetry and calligraphy, another between concrete poetry and the visual arts (it would be like the Italian idea of *poesia visiva*), another between concrete poetry and popular music (for instance, the lyrics of the Brazilian pop singer Gaetano Velhosa), and so on. Of course not all such intermedial works are fluxus works: the fluxus phenomenon appears when these works are treated as conceptual models, with no excess of *matière* involved in their realization. Such an excess could be either material or psychological or self-cognitive, but I will return to that presently.

However it is clear that such an approach, working from no assumptions about media, that the work assumes only that it will create its own inherent and natural medium, involves from the outset a certain measure of syncretism which was unusual in Western art for a long time immediately preceding this century—but which does in fact have a long and respectable lineage, so much so, in fact, that the Aristotelian tradition of rather discrete and inflexible genres and media could be judged a deviation (and perhaps an unfortunate one) from the mainstream. For instance, from the thick of the Aristotelian hysteria, what are the implications of this 1840 passage from the Scottish Thomas Carlyle, in his *On Heroes, Hero-Worship, and the Heroic in History?* "A *musical* thought is one spoken by a mind that has penetrated into the inmost heart of the thing; detected the inmost mystery of it, namely the *melody* that lies hidden within it; the inward harmony of coherence which is its soul, whereby it exists, and has a right to be, here in this world. All inmost things, we may say, are melodious; naturally utter themselves in Song. The meaning of Song goes deep."[1]

Carlyle's remark could have been made by a dadaist in some more rational moment. But tracing such a thought back in time, we find Coleridge saying something quite similar of poetry (since his art centered on poetry) in 1814: "All the fine arts are different species of poetry. The same spirit speaks to the mind through different senses by

[1]Thomas Carlyle, *Sartor Resartus/On Heroes and Hero-Worship* (New York: Dutton Everyman's Library, 1908), pp. 316–17.

manifestations of itself, appropriate to each. They admit therefore of a natural division into poetry of language (poetry in the emphatic sense, because less subject to the accidents and limitations of time and space); poetry of the ear, or music; the poetry of the eye."[2]

Before this, the Schlegels and Novalis had already voiced this idea in the aphorisms in the *Athenaeum;* but they may have been prompted to do so by the revival of interest in the ideas of Giordano Bruno (1548?–1600), about whom their friend Schelling wrote one of his major philosophical texts. Bruno is one of the most syncretic of all major thinkers, trying to find conceptual and linguistic patterns among all areas of intellectual concern in his time—magic, astrology, theology, ethics, epistemology, logic, mathematics, mythology, cosmology, and, of course, the arts. The last work published in his lifetime constitutes a veritable semiotics of some of these areas. Here is a quote from his *De Imaginum, Signorum, et Idearum Compositione* (1591): "Therefore, and in a certain measure, philosophers are painters; poets are painters and philosophers; painters are philosophers and poets. He who is not a poet and a painter is no philosopher. We say rightly that to understand is to see imaginary forms and figures; and understanding is fancy, at least it is not deprived of fancy."[3]

Of course the last part of the quotation deals with potential and the ability to conceive of an accurate model, not with idle daydreaming. But be that as it may, the track does not stop there. It goes back through Bernardus Silvestris of Chartres (fl. ca. 1150) and the syncretic impulse can even be found in the *De Institutione Musica . . .* of Boethius at the end of the fifth century: "Sed illud quidem, quod in instrumentis positum est ibique totam operam consumit, ut sunt citharoedi quique organo ceterisque musicae instrumentis artificium

---

[2]Samuel Taylor Coleridge, "On the Principles of Genial Criticism," in *Biographia Literaria,* ed. John Shawcross (London: Oxford University Press, 1907), 2: 220–21.

[3]Trans. in Isabel Frith, *Life of Giordano Bruno the Nolan,* rev. Moriz Carriere. (Boston: Ticknor, 1887), p. 16.

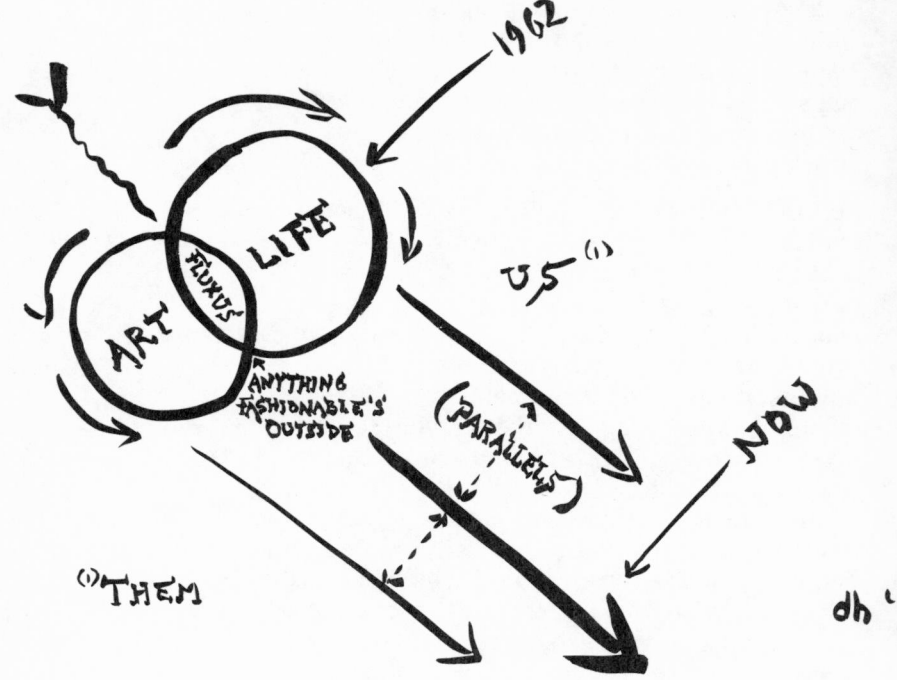

probant, a musicae scientiae intellectu seiuncti sunt, quoniam famulantur, ut dictum est: nec quicquam afferunt rationis, sed sunt totius speculationis expertes. Secundum vero musicam agentium genus poetarum est, quod non potius speculatione ac ratione, quam naturali quodam instinctu fertur ad carmen.''[4]

Here we are picking up a Pythagorean theme, that music can be a form of speculation on the principles of things—*musica speculativa* could be not just for performance but for metaphysical consideration. This idea lasted well into the Renaissance and only died out in the days of Johannes Kepler and Robert Fludd. But it is interwined in Boethius, in Saint Augustine's writings on music earlier in the fifth century, and through the Greek theoreticians of music and aesthetics, Aristoxenus and Nicomachus, to Plato (the *Timaeus*) and beyond.

[4]Anicius Manlius Torquatius Severinus Boetius, *De Institutione Arithmetica Libri Duo De Institutione Musica Libri Quinque,* ed. Gottfried Friedlein (1867; Frankfurt am Main: Minerva G.M.B.H., 1966), pp. 224–25.

In other words, it is a peculiarity of the recent past that anyone should think that concept art (concept music?), to use the 1961 term of the fluxartist Henry Flynt, was not among the obvious possibilities, or to imagine that the media of the arts were discrete. In fact one aspect of the fluxus focus is concretion of all kinds—the interpenetration of art and life as well as the interpenetration of the media.

But in terms of the particular cultural environment in which fluxus arose, fluxus was certainly not unique in its concern with the tracing of parallel patterns among media. For instance, it came about in the late 1950s. But in the late 1950s structuralism was also evolving, with its application of linguistic ideas taken from Saussure and Jakobson to the fields of anthropology (Levi-Strauss), psychology (Lacan), literature (Barthes), and so on. Whatever the feuds and splits among those who belong to the older orthodoxy of structuralism or those who belong to the newer one of poststructuralism (Derrida, Laplanche, Eco, Lyotard—even, way to one side in the computer department, Bense)—they are all influenced by their objects of study into common concerns with patterning and conceptual structures which are oddly analogous to fluxus considerations, though without the stripped-down-to-minimum model quality which fluxus *always* demands of its works if they are to exist as fluxus works. In fluxus as in mathematics, elegance consists in having enough and only enough to make the essence of a work or presentation absolutely clear. And elegance is a very desirable quality.

Fluxus is then, among other things, a kind of work, a form of forms, a metaform. As such, a fluxus thing is something that you can do as an artist—and when you do it you are being a fluxartist. But you are also free to do other things which may or nor relate to your fluxus work. The identity which the artist gets from doing a fluxus work is, then elusive, transitory as a flower's colors. If one is looking to one's art as a means of extending the personality, fluxus is a terrible place to look. It always lies outside the ego, except for parody or for metapsychological considerations.

Thus the big guns who, over the years, have climbed aboard the bandwagon hoping for prestige and said, "*I* was fluxus in 1954 (or 1957, or 1936, or whatever)" have produced virtually no memorable fluxus work—no work which could project beyond their personal stamp, beyond their charisma or their autograph. And thus the illusion of anonymity in fluxus: actually, if one sees a work by a fluxartist like George Brecht or Ben Vautier, it isn't really anonymous, once one has the expertise to distinguish. Brecht notices this kind of thing, typically, and Vautier notices that. But what is missing is the self-stereotyping of mannerism and personal expression (again, as in the case of many of Vautier's works, excepting the element of parody and humor—"I, Ben Dieu [= Bon Dieu, Good God] sign EVERYTHING!"). Self-cognition is not the point.

But this is increasingly, in our world culture, an age where self-cognition is not the point. Capitalism and industrial society created a cult of the strong individual opposed to The Masses, and a strong individual had to develop his sense of unique identity. The arts reflected this. In this new age of ours, in order to survive we must cooperate in many efforts: thus our focus is on the tasks at hand, and worrying too much about who or what we are would decrease our comfortable survival. Thus we tend to get our identities from what we do: the president of the republic, when he washes the dishes, is a dishwasher. And our question is no longer "Is it right for *me* to do this thing" (whatever it is) but "Is this thing something which needs doing? And which of my selves is to do it?" We are then, in a sense, postself-cognitive, or as I call it, for short, "postcognitive." This is the postcognitive era (following the postmodern one?), and fluxus is the realistic art of the postcognitive era to the extent that it reflects the concerns and essence of its era more fully than a more mimetic or an expressive art could.

Viewed in this light, some of the questions I raised or implied in art history become somewhat altered. In the first place, fluxus is not really a movement: its movement aspect is only metaphor, because it did not happen as a result of a group of people consciously coming together with common aims and objectives, with a program of introducing this or that tendency into the ongoing continuity of the arts. Rather it arose more or less spontaneously, was coordinated primarily by George Maciunas's naming it, and its various manifestations (performances and festivals, publications and exhibitions) have been surfacings of an ongoing activity rather than being the object of a professional and wholly committed, career-oriented strategy. A professional fluxist would be a bad fluxist. This contrasts diametrically with surrealism, where Pope André Breton could read people in or out of the movement at will, and where the artifacts which the surrealists produced were what they were trying to live from or off. It could be said that they parasitized their own movement. In this way surrealism was utterly self-cognitive, was indeed a movement—and the various fights and denunciations, which so much resemble the pecking of pigeons at a feast of crumbs, were quite inevitable.

On the other hand, futurism and dada were more like fluxus. Futurism was also a movement, but for all Marinetti's egocentrism, he did not claim the souls and blood of his associates. Futurism was a spirit as much as a body of achievement—and the vitality of the work, some seventy years after it was produced, speaks to the viewer in a way which quite transcends the individuality of the artist. Dadaism was not a movement—and its collapse was partly due to the attempt to make a movement out of it in the sense that surrealism later became one. Dada was a spirit, intuitive and counterrational, and the dada objects were merely the manifestations of that spirit. Thus futurism and dada can be said to be closer to fluxus than surrealism was in a way that is quite apart from the stylistic differences or similarities. All four are syncretic—but the element of spirit in general is greatest in dada and fluxus, and the similarity between these two is closest. Fluxus is, however, potentially rational where dada is not: dada allows only the irrational and anarchic. Fluxus allows any conceptual patterning, from the quietly intuitive (Mieko Shiomi's vanishing smile) to the mathematical permutation (Maciunas's *In*

Memoriam Adriano Olivetti) to the completely
aleatorical (the text pieces of myself or Jackson
Mac Low). And though dada and futurists works
may be minimal (e.g., the synthetic theater pieces
of Marinetti and others), only fluxus insists upon
this particular elegance, or vanishes without it.
And, in this case like surrealism, the sensibility so
derived is so clear and evident that fluxus can
claim works for itself from other times and places.
Let me close, then, with a fluxus poem by
Giordano Bruno, "Salomon & Pythagoras"—

> Quid est quod est?
> Ipsum quod fuit.
> Quid est quod fuit?
> Ipsum quod est.
> Nihil sub sole novum.[5]
> Jordani Bruni
> Nolani Wittenberg
> 8 Martij 1588

This translates—

> What is that is?
> The same that was.
> What is that was?
> The same that is.
> Nothing new under the sun.
> Giordano Bruno
> from Nola Wittenberg
> 8 March 1588

[5]Virgilio Salvestrini, *Bibliografia di Giordano Bruno
(1582–1950),* ed. Luigi Firpo, 2d posthumous ed. (Firenze:
Sansoni Antiquariato, 1958), p. 172.

11 The Poem within the Poem

A caveat: in talking about the chain of ideas which follows, it is almost impossible to present that chain except in its simplest forms—maxims and policies. And these will resemble statements of fact, dogma, or articles of belief. But they are not that: they are merely working hypotheses. They cannot be proved by any Euclidean means on which we would agree; their proof requires a geometry of life which may never exist. Thus, hopefully, the pontifical tone can be seen for what it is—a means of linking the elements of the chain. The reader must verify it himself, and even if all the links should prove to be false, perhaps the result will be some reader's providing a new chain which can make this one obsolete. This is my challenge, and if it is taken up, then the making of this chain will not have been in vain even if it is useless or obsolescent itself.

Poetry is normally a language art—not that there aren't poetries which are minimally linguistic (e.g., Richard Kostelanetz's poems in which all the units are numbers), but most draw on those codes which we see or hear as conveyors of meaning according to rules and conventions which we have learned. "Also" is an adverb suggesting "in addition" in English. "Also" is an adverb suggesting "therefore" in German. We look at a page, and it says "also." Our experience indicates that the rest of the page is also in English, not German. So we read the page as English; I'll return to this later, for there is more. But for now, we start by seeing the words on the page as conveyors of meaning in English.

We see the shapes and details of the letters; the poem reaches us through the eye. Some poetries trope on this more than others. Or we hear the sounds on the page—an array of verbs and vowels and appropriate sentence melodies—some poetries are very close to music and some are less so. Their value lies not in how many things they are close to but in what they are themselves. Our experience of these words is only partly derived from our previous readings of poetry; mostly it comes from their utilitarian uses in everyday life. People used to meet Gertrude Stein, whose use of language in her work is so very idiosyncratic, and wonder that she did not speak in the style she used when she wrote—yet, if she had not spoken rather normally, there would be no freshness to her use of daily words in so special a way in her writing: the contrast is part of the poetic style. But also, from these utilitarian uses of the words which are later used in poems, we make up our own horizons of what they mean or come to mean, which we later contrast and compare with the uses of the same words in a poem—this is important.

There is no need to define poetry, though I did so in the Glossary to this book. Some poet will always write a poem which does not match our favored definition, and we will rule it out only at the expense of narrowing our horizons and losing our poetic interest in this poet's work. But for our purposes here let us use not an ironclad definition but an emanating point of reference: a poem is what we experience by means of a verbal artifact, reaching the mind through eyes and ears, conveying the horizons of the poet—his times and moments of life and purposes, his sense of language, and his aesthetic. The poem is not the artifact, or not *just* the artifact: we must experience the artifact as a poem for it to become one. Left by itself it is just a verbal cipher, like a text in a language one does not know, which looks like it *ought* to be a poem, but who of us can say that's what it is? One does not know its code. But when one knows the code, one says: "let's see if this is what I think it is, a poem." And one proceeds. Our act of recognition transforms the artifact itself; we have chosen to treat it as a poem, and so it tends to become one. A logician might argue here that my reasoning is circular, but there are ways out of that and I invite him to find them. We have other paths to follow.

A poem is not its information or its meaning. We can strongly disagree with the overt and separable meaning of a poem—a hymn to a god we do not know, a praise of a political system we detest. But these are merely ways in which our horizons match the horizons of the poet without coinciding with them. We note his horizons and we feel them out. We experience the fitting and the nonfitting; the poet structured the experience according to his horizon, and we know ours fit us. Thus the meaning and the information are parts of the experience, integral to them—structural elements, part of their conceptual grammar.

The poem is not its look or sound. The poem may be set up conventionally with lines, smooth margins on the left and rough on the right. It may have its elements scattered on the page, or arrayed mimetically into recognizable shapes or nonmimetically into abstract forms or with all the elements following the meaning in one-to-one intensifiers. Those are parts of the horizon of the poet, to which we match our own. But the life of the poem is how we take it, not how it is. The sound may be virtually all the poet has allowed himself in that one poem—it may be a simple or a complex music, perhaps one only capable of being presented by means of a phonograph record or a tape, far far away from a row of typed words on a page; it may transcend any one or more of the earth's languages. But if it evokes these, using words as conveyors of meaning and significance to create its horizons, to that extent it is useful for us to treat it as a poem, to match its horizons with our own.

The poem is not its allusions, its images and metaphors. Some we recognize and some we miss; the loss is only ours. We try to see them all, but inevitably there are opacities along the poem's horizon, some blanks we sense are there and some which we do not even suspect. Is it less a poem for this? No, though we may be annoyed if the poet seems to want to call undue attention to this or that part of the process. These allusions have other purposes, however, one chief one of which is to evoke parts of our experience and horizons which we would not otherwise have thought up, and to set its connotations in parallel with those of the poem, to butress its impact. Of course this too is a structural element, but it is one which often strengthens the impact of the poem. Say the poem is in English and it swings into

Latin—if I read Latin, my experience of Latin poetry, my feelings about the Latin language itself, are called forth to add to the strength of the poem. Say the poem invokes another poem, quotes it or alludes to it; if I know that poem, my experience of it too is added to my experience of the poem. Say it alludes to my own experience of the springtime (I am thinking of e. e. cummings's "spring is like a perhaps hand/arranging and rearranging," I think of store windows and hands appearing, moving the items in the window around. Someone else might think of something else being alluded to; but each of us had had his horizons invoked, summoning up more of them into the matching process. If William Carlos Williams, in his *Paterson,* tells of a grey-eyed lady on the street, I think not just of grey-eyed ladies on the street but grey-eyed Athena, since that is so often Homer's epithet for her—and whether or not Williams intended I should do so pales beside the fact that I *do* do so, will I or nill I. Since I am reading not just to discover Williams's horizons alone, which would be an academic exercise of, to me, no great value (not being a biographer of Williams, say), but to experience the poem, since it seems to fit and is not canceled back off again by disappearing or by subsequent appearance of some which would overpower the "grey-eyed" epithet—say, by being told that her mascara was grey as well, since I do not imagine Athena wearing mascara, I assume that Williams is quite probably, in fact, alluding to Athena. Again, Milton's lines are filled with allusions to myths that I do not know—so many of them that their presence colors the quality of the works. Would it bother me that he might have slipped in a few whom he had invented himself? Not in the least: the process of the mythological allusions is as important as the allusions themselves—the names people the poems as much as do the myths, and the qualities of the names are part of the horizons. Similarly, to choose a poet of the recent past, Charles Olson in *Maximus* constantly refers to the local history of Gloucester, Massachusetts, and Worcester, Massachusetts. Need I know every name and place referred to? No. Within the poem, I can trust Olson—his horizon comes from the process and the sense of place which it evokes. In fact I once noticed a point where he has misremembered a detail of the geography of Worcester, a town where I spent much of my childhood. Yes—it introduces a false note for me, but not a very serious one. It's no worse than a birthmark on the cheek of someone I have loved. I might wish it gone, but it is part of how a face is, so if I would love the face, the birthmark goes along with it.

A poem is not its language. It can be translated—never exactly, of course, but something of it reappears in the new language. The horizon is shifted, relocated. The poem can be paraphrased—made again in its own language, keeping just the senses or the sounds but using all different words. For the paraphrased text, the new one is monitored by the old, so the old one becomes a structural element. I may well enjoy comparing the new and old versions, the translation and the original. New horizons have been created. Again, in some cases the reader of a poem is more or less obliged to make a paraphrase himself. Take the Shakespearean line, "A true conceipt of godlike Amity." The words and uses in such a line are so unconventional that a reader, confronted by it, tends to make a quick paraphrase for himself, something like: "a real expression of divine/impersonal/objective friendship." The paraphrase, once made, is forgotten; but the justification for the Shakespearean line is not just that it is beautiful itself, but lies in its very displacement from the norms of language—the fact that it is beautiful and makes the reader or hearer *want* to paraphrase it in order to understand its overt meaning, that is an element in the horizon presented in the line. By presenting lines like this the poet keeps the reader active. Too many of them and the reader would be stunned into insensibility, would be exhausted. Too few and the reader will become passive, letting the lines carry him or her along with only part of his horizon-matching capability engaged.

A poem is not its significance, which changes with every age and indeed from the vantage point of every reader. These significances are important, to

within the
Poem
105

be sure: the poet's time, the poem's time, the editor's time, the type designer's time, the reader's time (both historical and in terms of his own life and maturity), these are all part of what makes up the horizon-matching process. But how they change! The poem which we passed over yesterday is the favorite of today. The poem which we once ignored is called to our attention by other poems which we encounter; we see some measure of influence, which retroactively colors the original so that, like the subject on a microscope slide, the new stain brings out elements we had not noticed and new significance is given to the old poem. The critic convinces us. Or perhaps we ourselves grow to be some new persons or people, and the old significance is lost—our taste improves, we come to know something better, and that whole horizon shifts as well.

No, all these things which *the poem* is not are vectors, lines of force compelling our horizons and the implied horizon of the text into a process of matching, and the poem is this passionate and intellectual co-fusion experience. Thus, if we are to analyze a poem we must, to put it as a paradox, look for the poem within the poem, the poem within the text, the language, the significance, the meaning, the allusions and the language; we must identify all those vectors, including our own as well as those of the poet and of any intermediary between the poet and ourselves (translator, editor, or whatever).

The poet's craft is the means by which the poet fuses his own horizons with those of an implied reader by means of his artifact, his poem. He makes certain assumptions about the reader's previous reading—does the reader know the texts to which the poet alludes? He shares with the reader elements of his own life and language experience. He provokes the reader, tries to call the reader to new life and sensibilities—thus the ongoing appeal to the poet of the new and innovative, but thus also the appeal to the poet of finding his own form in unnoticed ways in works of his past experience: "I have made Shakespeare *mine* by using him, by showing how like him I can be" (or if not Shakespeare, the Donne or Raleigh or whatever master one chooses to transform and to apply). There are the dangers: the meaning may be opaque and lose its structuring and monitoring function, the sound of the poem or its look may be either too striking or too monotonous, the language may be so bizarre as to become numbing or so flat as to become monotonous, the urge to invest the poem with significance may lead to historicity or self-conscious gesturing. But above all the poet makes the poem an active point for the horizons—his own and those of his implied reader. Every poem is a world, with all its inherent frustration and beauty.

One technical element is worth a short digression here. It is the element of displacement, so necessary in a work (not just a poem) if it is not to be entirely bland and lacking in impact. Elsewhere I have called it the "allusive referential."* This clumsy term merely signifies how the process of alluding to a reality by placing it in a work of art displaces our perception of it from where we might have expected it (and how) to where we now perceive it (and how). The Shakespearean line I cited is an example of an allusive referential. In practice, if one has decided to try the horizons approach, most of one's attention is taken in watching this process of displacement through the work. One sees A, which corresponds to B in one's own world: one now experiences C. It is this displacement which keeps the process from being a mere cerebral exercise—which gives the work its impact on the gut level and in its intellectual appeal.

But to return to my main argument, in a situation such as I have described, the reader is a co-poet, since the poem does not exist until it is read, either to oneself or aloud or by someone else. Each of these has its advantages, some more for some poems and some for others. The reader, the hearer, the performer, these may be the same person: that is not the point. But in each case the receiver of the poem (reader, hearer, or performer) must have the skills to match the work, most know what is in the text enough to perform it, read it, or

---

*"Towards an Allusive Referential," in A Dialectic of Centuries, 2d ed. (New York: Printed Editions, 1978).

hear it meaningfully. Thus the problem is to work toward the making of a great reader. We cannot all be great poets in the sense of fashioning and articulating poems which have sufficient strength to produce powerful experiences of the horizon. But the great reader is the ordinary man or woman who has learned to bring his or her horizon to the text to produce a great experience, who can concentrate his or her awareness enough to cause a text to be perceived with all its significances and implications for heart and mind, to bring it alive. It does not matter what is the source of a poem; some poets have even done "found poems," finding a text in the course of their workaday experience, noticing it more or less intact, and claiming it for and re-presenting it as a work. W. C. Williams included a shopping list in *Paterson* as an example of this. Bern Porter is a poet who has done large books on such found texts. When a poet does this, he is offering us a paradigm of his art as greater reader—seeing the text's potential where it would not normally be expected, and offering it to us as a new entity. Drawing on this experience when we return to normative, made, and written-out poetry, we see the process is no different; the poet gives us the text, and the great reader creates it significance as much as ever the poet did. If there is any utilitarian value in the reading of poetry, perhaps it lies here: co-creating the poem develops our minds and makes them flexible, which changes us perhaps therapeutically. Isn't that one of the aims of education at its best? To teach us, in general, to think? To be able to draw upon our own experiences and horizons to create new situations and potentials? The poem which provokes this need not be thanked; it is merely doing its job.

12 From a Letter to Steve McCaffery (3 October 1977)

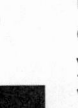

. . . I do not agree with your defense of Derrida but am very interested by it; I've looked through a copy of *Glas* but haven't yet gotten one for my very own chewing. As for his vocabulary, If I say

THIS SENTENCE IS INCONSISTENT

does that either make it inconsistent? Or does it make some discussion of which it is a part *more* consistent? True, I like the paradox involved in saying such a thing. But I don't think it solves any of the problems . . .

Probably I should simply postpone (again) any discussion on my part of the Paris Mafia—I do think the reference is useful and not just amusing or satirical; for the last year I've been reading bushels of books in the area—two fine Jonathan Culler books, Bense, and Heissenbüttel (have you seen his three little lollypops from *Diana's Bimonthly* ("Novel," "Schematic Development of Tradition," and "The Dilemma of Being High and Dry"—$1 each), Jakobson—parts of whose theory I like—and Barthes, Eco, Derrida, Lacan, and Lyotard, among whom familiarity brings an increasing perception of similarities. I agree that the implications of these gents for new art and writing haven't been followed through except in a minor way (e.g., Maurice Roche), but to do so would seem to me to be very after-the-fact— "thin-making," to allude to your phrase in your letter.

But ah, to sign the sign (and humanize it), to stress the direct and indirect signified—you are quite right, that is the teleology of my allusive referential idea and should be the purpose of my quest, not to fret over the teleological confusion of the Paris Brethren. (Notice: virtually no women among them—why?) Furthermore, you've pointed up some confusion of my own, for which I thank thee.

Do I see a structural primacy in my poems, you ask: no, I see a constant dialectic on as many levels as possible. Hence my attraction to Ramus and Bruno. Hence my "intermedia" notion. Hell, it even affects my sexuality. I am attracted and moved by multi-hattedness, and the forms I employ reflect this. E.g., in *classic plays* and in the new *Everyone Has Sher Favorite (His and Hers)* and elsewhere there are many poems in what I call my "snowflake" form—visually symmetrical, with the visual structure tied to the semantic sense and thus in constant interplay. Example:

those pieces

that move like this

those pieces

i say

are snowflakes

i say

those pieces

that move like this

those pieces

They are symmetrical visually and conceptually: the form falls apart (i.e., it seems silly) when it is used abstractly—either nonsemantically or acoustically à la sound poetry (it seems arbitrary), but when the snowflake is in dialectic with content, it tends to feel quite natural. Similarly, there's a form I've used a lot since "moments in the lives of great women" and before (in *foew&ombwhnw*) where the form is simply a triangle, a rectangle or a pair of triangles:

a short
line must be
followed by much longer
lines until a strong visual shape results

The triangle or triangles can go either way:

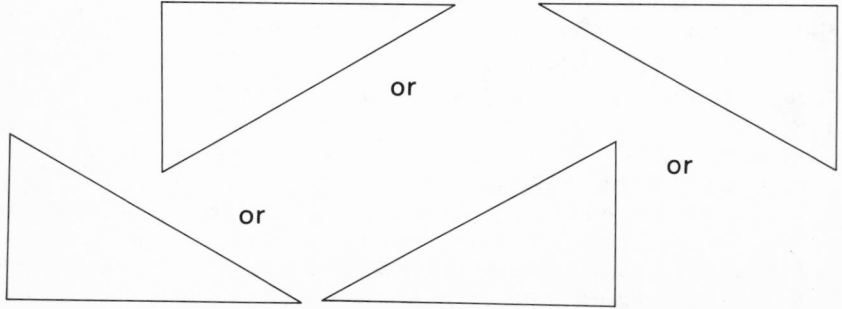

Of course my example is just that: I almost never carry an idea from one line into the next *except* to create momentum or for variation—I like to use the length for its own sake, certainly à la George Herbert in his "Easter Wings" and à la one kind of W. C. Williams. The triangle form implies two kinds of rectangles also:

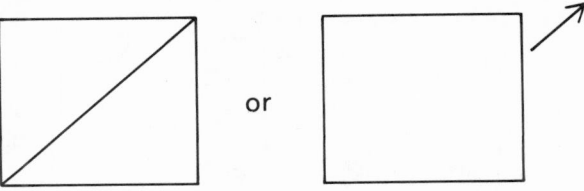

subjectively the diagonal can feel like it's outside.

The two triangles form one, and the exact repeats from another:

bbbbbbbb   the long one is very clear
abbbbbbb   is the short?
aabbbbbb   is the short?
aaabbbbb   is the short?
aaaabbbb   or   is the short?
aaaaabbb   is the short?
aaaaaabb   is the short?
aaaaaaab   is the short?
aaaaaaaa   the long one is very clear

The stasis of the second kind seems to work best when it is in contrast with something quite different before or afterward.

Finally, the triangles can align to form a rhombus or a parallelogram:

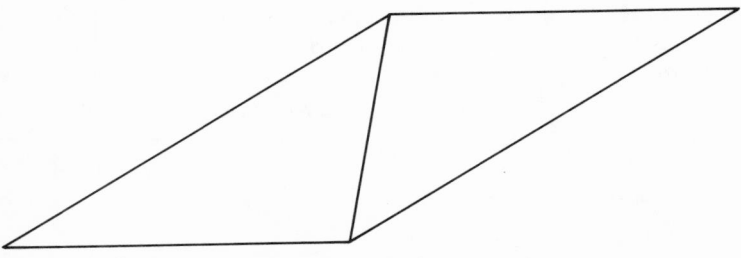

And/or the rhombus can be presented or imitated with right angles only (which relates to the second kind of rectangle also), or a series of these kinds of structures can be nested, the one inside the other, to give a sort of caryatid if it is extended on and on, which could in most cases project on to infinity à la *Brancusi's* sculptures.

Obviously such caryatids can either repeat the same form exactly (as in the right-hand example), or they can follow some modular progression of their own (as in the left-hand example). *So:* as the term "structure" is used by traditional literary critics, I doubt the shapes are structures. But as "structure" is used by art historians—e.g., *Michel Seuphor* in his critiques in the 1940s and 1950s of geometric abstract painting—they are indeed structures. So am I "structure-oriented?" Among other things, yes. But I don't think it's as mean ingful to call me that as "process-oriented" —the process of allusion and reference interests me far more than either signifiers or signified (or any other *thing*), and the active process of relation between language and meaning, form and content, structure and reference, is much more interesting to me than either polarity. I just ain't the *pure* type . . .

13 six trivial reflections

i

i am saying. i am saying that i am saying.

saying that, i am:

i am:

in-saying, out-saying, through-saying, and proto-saying
are signs of in-being, out-being, through-being and proto-being.

but in saying, i am hearing. hearing what i have said,
actually and potentially.

in-hearing, out-hearing, through-hearing and proto-hearing.

if i had not heard, i could not say.

the more fully i have said, the more fully i can hear.

i can say expressively, i can hear expressively.

but only when i agree with myself what expression is and
what it is not. this gives a history. the making of models.

ii

having received a model, there now exists a you-model
as well as an i-model—i received it as i gave it.

and an it-model proceeds from both. but it lacks some
attributes of you and me—our potential sexuality for one: thus
a he-it and a she-it. life things having sexuality?

the star alive? the planet alive? the fig and the stone
alive? at least as metaphor.

and a which-model and a that-model. the thing

perceived before it is understood, and the thing perceived
once it is understood. understanding understanding, including
the model of understanding. this last, such a complex organism,
like a living body: but so simple to take whole.

model-making exists. model-matching exists.

to conceive and to perceive.

iii

suggested improvement for theology:

in the beginning god conceived the heavens and the earth.

in the beginning god perceived the heavens and the earth.

in the beginning god conceived and perceived himself.

example: "who told you that you were naked?"

iv

art: model-making and model-using.

conceptive and perceptive art: art.

in practice: also model-improving and model-worsening,
healing and sickening, instructing and oblivifying.

nietzsche: "there are no moral phenomena, only the moral
perceptions of phenomena."

ditto for beauty, ditto for importance: "beautiful" and
"important" in nietzsche's remark.

making one's own further examples.

v

goethe: "everything is a symbol."

implies this or that, points hither or yon. the "universe
in a blade of grass" truism.

yet code of symbols can be usefully treated as a
language. a work as a language. a body of works as a language.
a language as a language. a language of languages.

the word within the language, and the sentence within the
language. sentences, paragraphs and larger mid-units. conceptual
non-structural units: transforms.

change all the *paroles* of a *langue,* and to what extent is
it still the same *langue*?

change all the *paroles* of the work of art, and to what
extent is it still the same work of art?

systems of *paroles* that are transcendent to them: matrices
within the *langue*—form. form and *trans*-form. implicit in the
model approach? form as grammar in a work? quantitative form?

and the hermeneutic study of subjects or *paroles*?

art apart from thought or philosophy?

vi

If I sit, can I ask questions? And if I ask questions,
can I think? Why not figure out some of the answers?

a. Los Angeles? Its own Zen.

The only quiet Chinatown in the world. Two arcades.
People in duos, trios, quartets, quintets, up to octets.
Ocasionally speaking, their eyes never meeting.

Friday night, The cars in the street gliding like big
tin bats. Never fluttering.

Hot. An office in a plastic Mexican colonial style,
opposite an open-air squash court. Biff boff. Office door
open. Vacant topped desk. Lovely oriental girl staring
off into space. Hands resting on synthetic teak. Elsewhere,
a sign which would usually read "Miss Yang" or "Eleanor
Fujikawa" or some such. In Los Angeles, reading simply "someone."
Biff boff.

b. Look, Ma. No verbs, except as participles, infinitives,
imperatives. No indicative: nothing to indicate. Nothing
strongly indicated.

Why?

Why not?

Writing as picture. Sometimes as sound. Meaning by
embodying. By embedding.

In the silence of North America, so natural to be a
painter or composer or concept artist (con-plus-septic). So
foreign to write with the mind's own music.

Take yer picture, Mister? Guaranteed 100 percent organically
grown words.

Friday: Mergenthaler Linotype announcing no more
hot Linotype machines. Only Linofilm. Write yer picture,
Mister? Americans taking pictures of letters. *Othmar
Mergenthaler*, German mechanical genius, at home with his
wife, hot molten metal. *Niebelungenliedergrafik.* Now
settled in Baltimore among the Liederkranzes. Now dying
young in a land without much hot stuff metal.

Cool. Take yer picture, Mister? Chemicals, raped
from landscape. Writing to be photolettered too. Why so
little concrete poetry in North America? Why so much other
visual poetry? Protocalligraphy (often typewritten)? Nearbeat
visual stuff? Near beer? Take yer picture, Mister?

Why so little structure?

At General Motors? Structural reflections of Economic
Anarchy? The Monolithic Anarchism of General Motors or an
American Art College? *Talcott Parsons*? *Bucky Fuller's* snapshots
of his yacht. *Hermann Kahn.* Take yer picture, Mister?

C. Cheeses? Pleases Jesus.
   Jesus Pieces pleases.*
   Jesus pieces pleases.
   Cheeses pieces pleases.
   Jesus Pieces pleases Jesus.
   Cheeses pleases Jesus.
   Cheeses pieces Jesus.
   Pieces Jesus cheeses?

Jesus piecing cheeses? Hear or seen. Much more real
than directed to the mind. Who?—keeping us so mindless.
Whose interests being served?

---

*Jesus Pieces is the village in England where I was born. But
my point is proved by the fact that knowing this adds nothing
whatever to the text.

15 The Strategy of Each of My Books

What Are Legends (1960), my first book, is the theoretical text which goes with *Legends and Fishnets* (1958–60, 1969; published in 1976). It exemplifies my near-obsession with unifying my theory and practice, written as it is in my "legend" style; this style uses few verbs in the indicative mode, substituting participles wherever possible, in order to get a pictorial effect in words. Important conceptual models to me were certain late Latin poems in which strings of participles provide the movement of the poem (e.g., the "Stabat Mater") and the last part of the De Quincey "English Mail Coach," as well as the obvious modernist texts by Gertrude Stein and others. I printed it myself when I was at the Manhattan School of Printing, using a handlettered text and found-illustrations by Bern Porter, a highly original graphic artist and writer from Maine whose work I have admired for many years.

Jefferson's Birthday/Postface (1964) is two books, bound back to back. *Jefferson's Birthday* includes all the texts which I composed between April 13, 1962 (Thomas Jefferson's birthday) and April 13, 1963. The book came about when George Maciunas, the organizer of fluxus, offered to publish all my texts. I said it would be a monstrously big book, decidedly non-commercial. He then suggested that he publish a year's worth of my writings, which would then provide a cross-section of my work. I was delighted with the idea and proceeded to finish all texts begun during that year (which I seldom do). It is, in fact, representative of my work from that time except that it includes no long texts. The resulting manuscript then lay on his desk for several months, while he tried to make the peace with it.

His studio was downstairs from mine, and every few days I would drop by and ask him what was happening with it. He would stall and groan—it was much bigger than he had expected. Finally he told me that it would be ready "a year from next spring." That was too late, I said—I needed the books for acting scripts, etc. He said there was nothing he could do about that. I then went to the bar downstairs and had a few drinks, went back up to his studio, removed my manuscript and took it upstairs to my studio, returned to the bar and had a few more drinks. I then went home to Alison Knowles, a fluxus artist to whom I was married at the time.

"Alison," I said, "We've founded a press."

"Oh really," Alison said, startled. "What's it called?"

"Shirtsleeves Press," I said.

"That's no good," she said. "What don't you call it something else?" I thought about that, and the next day I wrote the "Something Else Manifesto," in which I promised always to publish "something else," different from whatever was in vogue at the time.

Postface is a rather personal memoir of the early days of happenings and fluxus in which, as I said before, I was active. I was aware that the pieces in *Jefferson's Birthday* would seem strange to most readers, so it was important to me to provide a context for those pieces—the essay is a little thin on theoretical content, but as narrative and polemic (attacking alternative, conventional modes of working) it was valuable enough that it will now (1981) be reissued by another publisher. As for Something Else Press, it lasted from 1964 to 1974 (I left it in 1973), and one aspect of it too was to provide a context for the understanding of my works—I always thought of it as a big collage with many contributors.

Throughout the later 1960s I brought out rather few of my own books—only the first canto of *A Book about Love & War & Death* (1960–70), which appeared in Something Else Press's inexpensive Great Bear Pamphlet series, as a sort of work-in-progress publication—more of that in a minute. Most of my creative work was in film, photography, and performance at that time, and a lot of my attention was devoted to working out a theoretical position which would be more appropriate to the avant-garde than the conventional, Aristotelian models with their emphasis on power (especially catharsis). The preliminary texts in this direction, such as the essay "Intermedia" (1963–64) which revived that term from Samuel Taylor Coleridge, were published and sent out free to friends of Something Else Press in the *Something Else Newsletter.* One of these essays from the *Newsletter* appeared also as a pamphlet, *Towards the 1970's* with another small press in 1969; in it I tried to predict (with mixed success) what would be of importance to those who followed the new arts in America in the 1970s—notably "a revolution in subject matter" which came true with the obsession with subject matter/meaning/narrativity in structuralism and semiotics (to which I was only partly sympathetic), and the new centrality of the dance to our arts (Meredith Monk and Trisha Brown, for example).

But by 1969 it was clear that I had to do a new cross-section of my work and to reissue the texts which had appeared in the *Newsletter,* some issues of which were becoming scarce. I therefore did *foew&ombwhnw* (1969), which is, ironically, bound as a prayer book. The book is in four columns. The left-hand column continuously features long works, mostly for performance, such as the Danger Music series or the long aleatoric play *St. Joan at Beaurevoir* (1958–59) with its long phonemic speech structures. The second column includes short plays and graphics. The third column is poetry, and the fourth column is essays—not only the *Newsletter* texts but also, for example, a long account of the *Graphis* series (1958–   ), a series of graphical notations for musical, theatrical, and other performances which is still a preoccupation of mine now, nearly a quarter century later. The design of the book reflects the McLuhanesque preoccupations of the time, with its simultaneities, but is also, to some extent a book about making a book, reflecting my experience doing almost all the design work for the Something Else Press.

Also in 1969 I brought out *Pop Architektur* with a trade publisher in Germany, a collection co-edited and designed with Wolf Vostell, a colleague from happenings and fluxus; the English text, slightly expanded, appeared in 1970 with Something Else Press as *Fantastic Architecture*. It is an anthology of ideas by artists and composers and writers about the elements of architecture—space, construction, environment—some practical and some fantastic, and with commentaries on some of the ideas of the artists or on the elements of architecture, printed on translucent sheets bound into the book; my commentaries are in the *Legend* style to make them literary works and not just traditional captions. Again, it was a matter of combining Theorie and Praxis in the German sense.

The same small press which had done *Towards the 1970's* also did two more pamphlets, *Die Fabelhafte Geträume von Taifun-Willi* in its original mixed German-and-English text (an all-German translation was done in 1969 by a small press in Stuttgart) and *Computers for the Arts,* both in 1970. *Willi* is the first of my radio plays—a supposed tape-recorded dialogue between two reporters at an impossibly large happening—and reflects my love of radio as a medium; I love the way radio allows us to imagine the visual element (which television so imperfectly realizes), providing us with a literature which one can experience while doing something else, while driving a car, for example. *Computers for the Arts* is a polemic in favor of the artist being his or her own technician; as information it is now very much out of date, but the point remains important to me, that collaboration often leads to diffused works with diluted personality.

By 1972 Something Else Press was no longer a small press. Two of its books had sold well over ten thousand copies, and I was running myself ragged raising funds to do new books, which was ruining my health. The history of Something Else Press is not a subject to investigate in depth here; I have told my side of the story in two long accounts in the *New Lazarus Review* (1979 and 1980) and there are two books about Something Else Press, Hugh Fox's *An Analytic Checklist of Something Else Press* (1974) and to much more comprehensive Peter Frank book, *Something Else Press: An Annotated Bibliography* (1983). What I missed was the flexibility of Something Else as a *small* press. So in 1972, at the suggestion of my friend and co-worker Nelleke Rosenthal, I started Unpublished Editions, in order to make model editions of my books, which would, hopefully, be reissued in time by trade publishers.

The first book from Unpublished Editions was *amigo* (1972), a series of gay love poems; it was also my first book of just poems as such, with no theoretical texts included.

Also in 1972 there appeared my last Something Else Press book, the complete *Book about Love & War & Death* (1960–70). As I mentioned before, the first canto had already appeared in 1965, and also the second and third cantos appeared with a small press in California, Nova Broadcast Express, which was edited by Jan Herman, my successor at Something Else Press. With half the work in print, it seemed desirable to do the rest of it, so I did. It is my largest published prose work, a sort of aleatoric novel with sections in poetry after the manner of some of the romantic writers of Germany, who have been a lifelong interest of mine; more of that presently.

The next Unpublished Editions book was *The Ladder to the Moon* (1959–63, rewritten and published in 1973), my largest work for the theater to date. It is a very opulent, romantic piece with sections (e.g., the "Tiger Lady Episode") in which the normal time progression is suspended; all my experience in happenings and fluxus is included in that work, and I will write no more large-scale theater works until *The Ladder* has been performed—I can't.

Also in 1973 Unpublished Editions brought out *For Eugene in Germany,* a sort of sequel to *amigo* but, somehow, dead; it is the only book I have done which I regret. In the same year two small publications appeared with small presses in Europe: *Gesehen, Gehört, und Verstanden,* from Reflection Press in Stuttgart (which had done the German version of *Willi*), which is a translation of an issue of the *Something Else Newsletter,* "Seen,

Heard, and Understood," a praise of the literary medium, and also *Le Petit Cirque au Fin du Monde,* a radio play in my French, which is pretty bad, a sort of homage à Jean Cocteau (whose "Le Printemps au Fond de la Mer" is a favorite of mine). Its only performance to date happened when it was on the desk of Jean-Jacques Lebel, a teacher at the University of Paris at Vincennes in May 1968 when the students seized the university; they broadcast it over the university intercom during the insurrection.

For me the big event of 1973 was finally leaving Something Else Press. I celebrated it by setting to work on a huge cycle of prints, *7.7.73,* which eventually numbered more than eight hundred graphic works, mostly silk screen, but which also extended into different media—sculptures and environments and even a visual diary which is, as yet, incomplete. The cycle was organized to follow the seasons of the year, and the climax was the spring, since I felt that I had reached a new springtime in my life. For the springtime I also took some of the better visual images, printed them onto plastic, and made up a set of shadow puppets and a nonstory to go around them. For these puppets I composed an opera, the libretto of which was published in 1973 (well before the cycle was complete) as *Spring Game* by Unpublished Editions.

Finally in 1974 there was the Unpublished Editions *City with All the Angles* (written in 1970–71), a radio play which satirizes Los Angeles where I was living (if it can be said that anyone really *lives* there) at the time I wrote it. That completed the cycle of radio literature which I wanted to make. I have written other works for radio, but they belong to another world. For example, there is the presently unpublished *Ebb Tide* (1975), but it belongs to the cycle of *amigo* and *For Eugene in Germany.*

In 1975 I collected my aleatoric and other system poems together, destroyed many of them, and published or republished the rest as *Modular Poems* with Unpublished Editions. Many of these had appeared in mimeographed form earlier, and others had been in little magazines, but I needed a substantial book of such poems to complement the more prose-oriented *Book about Love & War & Death*, if there were to be a cycle of aleatoric works that would be in any way a balanced statement by one artist of the possibilities in that area. Collecting these poems stimulated me to compose a new aleatoric cycle of poems, conceived as a set, so I wrote "The Colors" in March 1975; in 1977 it was accepted for publication by an Italian publisher, but it has never appeared. I feel this nonpublication as a gap.

My interest in languages other than my native English had been an ongoing preoccupation from the beginning, as the reader can see from the list of books to date. But I also, therefore, felt that I should extend this into a single work in two languages, punning back and forth between the two. So it happened that in 1976 I wrote and Unpublished Editions published *classic plays,* which is in French and English throughout, and the title of which is an ironically pretentious reference to *word*plays as well as an allusion to its story, the Persephone myth, which it tells by allusion and reference, following an idea of Augustus Wilhelm Schlegel, one of the Jena group of early German romantics, of whom more in a moment.

As yet, I had published rather few works of fiction, and so it was now time to bring out the whole set of works, *Legends & Fishnets* (1959–69) to which *What Are Legends* (1960) had been the prefatory statement. This Unpublished Editions did in 1976. At the same time a small press in California, Tuumba Press, brought out *Cat Alley* a very short novel which is in some ways a counterpart to *amigo* and which tells the story of an imagined affair between a married man and his secretary; it is the same story that is told in "Moments in the Lives of Great Women," the longest poetic work in *foew&ombwhnw* (1969).

Returning to the language investigations again, in 1977 Studio Morra in Naples, Italy, where I had a show of ceramic shards on which their texts were drawn in calligraphy, brought out *The Epitaphs/Gli Epitaphi,* satirical epigrammatic poems in Latin,

French, German, and Swedish. It is poorly edited but handsome.

But apart from *7.7.73*, the decade of the 1970s was, for me, principally my decade as a poet. I therefore decided to publish two books of poems, the first a miscellany and the second a more concentrated, highly visual selection. The first was published by Unpublished Editions as *Everyone Has Sher Favorite (His or Hers)*, and it ends with a story showing my poetic techniques applied to fiction. The second, *some recent snowflakes (and other things)* (1979) ends in the same way, but we shall get to it in due course.

In 1974–75 I suffered a severe nervous breakdown which left me without much sense of who I was. I therefore enrolled in the Graduate English Department at New York University in order to inventory the English-language literature which was of interest to me, to find my roots and precedents, and to improve my scholarly habits. One preoccupation which emerged from this investigation was old visual poetry—the ancestors to the concrete poetry of the 1950s and since, and of which I have been a desultory practitioner since the early days. I assembled a tremendous collection of such texts, nearly a thousand items from ca. 500 B.C. to A.D. 1900, my arbitrary cutoff date, in Greek, Latin, Hebrew, Arabic, Turkish, Chinese, Gujarati (an Indian language), Russian, Polish, German, Swedish, Czech, Serbo-Croatian, French, Dutch, Spanish, and Portuguese (among others), as well as English. Virtually no scholarship existed in this area, which flourished up to the end of the baroque period, and then "went underground" into folk and comic poetry, during the period of neo-Aristotelian art (ca. 1660–1960) until, at the beginning of this century, it began to come back into vogue with the works of Mallarmé, Apollinaire, the futurists, constructivists, and dadaists, etc. There was no way that I could focus upon this entire field—to do an anthology of all my findings was far beyond my means—so I instead concentrated upon some of the currents of the field that relate to the great English poet George Herbert (1593–1633), and in 1977 Unpublished Editions brought out my *George*

Herbert's Pattern Poems: In Their Tradition, a scholarly monograph whose bibliography, while itself quite selective, at least includes enough materials to suggest to comparative literature scholars what a lot of work has yet to be done in this very fertile field.

The Unpublished Editions project had been so successful for me that in 1975 I was joined in it by Alison Knowles, and in 1978 by John Cage, Philip Corner, Geoffrey Hendricks, Jackson Mac Low, and Pauline Oliveros (in 1980 Jerome Rothenberg also joined the group); the group, however, chose to change the name from Unpublished Editions to Printed Editions, which is its present monicker. The strategy of the books remains the same, however—to bring out model editions of one's less commercially viable work (which includes, evidently, virtually all of mine, according to the trade publishing establishment) and to sell them through a common catalog; someday, hopefully, the books will be reissued by commercial publishers. I still try every year to get such publishers interested in my work, but it never happens. The last time I did this, the trade publisher told me his sales force had estimated that they could sell perhaps 600 copies of a manuscript-book that I had offered him; and since, with (now) Printed Editions I can usually sell 1,000–1,500 copies of whatever I produce, this did not seem like a wise way to proceed.

Thinking about these problems induced me to write *The Epickall Quest of the Brothers Dichtung and Other Outrages,* my first Printed Editions book for 1978. The title story is the result of first writing a long essay on the narrative theory of two of the Jena group of German romantics, Friedrich and Augustus Wilhelm Schlegel while, simultaneously, reading John Bunyan's *Pilgrim's Progress.* I realized that there were probably only a dozen or so people in the world who would understand my essay, so I discarded it: but its traces remained in my mind. So I wrote, instead, a satirical novella about the American literary scene, interspersing many of the Schlegel brothers' ideas, and giving the whole the picaresque plot of two brother poets wandering toward Mount Parnassus. Also in the book is an account of European history seen in the microcosm of the croissant. My friend from fluxus, Ken Friedman, provided me with some delightful line drawings, and the result was one of my most accessible works.

But my most serious work for 1978 was the other Printed Editions book, *A Dialectic of Centuries: Notes Towards a Theory of the New Arts.* By now the *Newsletter* essays were out of print, and I had broadened my understanding of the dynamics of the new arts of which I was a part, by the ideas of exemplativism (the notion that a work can be a more or less arbitrary example chosen by the artist from a range of possibilities inherent in its conception), which attacks the idea, so prevalent till now, of definitiveness, and of the allusive referential, the concept that the displacement of what we *actually* hear or see from what we *expect* to hear or see can be a factor in giving the work its emotional context. It was therefore desirable to collect my present theory texts together in a book, which I therefore did. However it sold much better than I had expected, and I found myself virtually out of stock on it. At the same time, the original printing had been rather shoddy and there were a few inconsistencies in my thought which bothered me, so in 1979 I brought out a second, revised edition, which is where that book can stand. I will not reprint those *Newsletter* essays again, although ideas from them will surely reappear in later theoretical formulations.

Part of my desire to call attention to the new relevance of German romanticism was incomplete: many of the texts were unavailable in modern translations. In 1977, as part of my studies at New York University I was obliged to pass an examination in a foreign language. I chose German, and to brush up on my language, I made a translation of Novalis's *Hymne an die Nacht,* one of the masterpieces of the Jena phase of the movement. This was published by Treacle Press in 1978; there are, however, a few inaccuracies in it, and also I would like to complete my work in this area by making available some of the texts by the Schlegels which are the basis for my insistence on their relevance, so that is a project which is at hand.

Making available key works from the past, taking them away from the heavy hand of the specialists and bringing them into the light of the day—this is an ongoing theme in my literary activity. I had done it in Something Else Press days by republishing rare classics—the *Dada Almanach* (because so many people accused me of being a dadaist without having any idea what the dadaists had actually achieved), the more experimental works of Gertrude Stein (which were, in the 1960s, more "talked about than read," as she had once lamented during her lifetime)—we published *The Making of Americans, Lucy Church Amiably, Matisse, Picasso, and Gertrude Stein* (also known as *G.M.P.*), *How to Write, Geography and Plays,* and *A Book Concluding with As a Wife Has a Cow*—and, of interest to music people, Henry Cowell's very prophetic *New Musical Resources.* But this work was also incomplete; even though I had no ambitions as a scholar, it was necessary to establish my own context. So I decided to work on Giordano Bruno, and to translate some of his Latin writings, which are more interesting to the cultural historians than are the more familiar Italian ones, but none of which have been published in any modern language although Bruno died over 380 years ago. I did this in collaboration with Charles Doria, a classics scholar and poet, starting with his striking sixteenth-century semiotics, *On the Composition of Images, Signs, and Ideas.* Selections from our translation have appeared in a California magazine, *Wch Wy,* but the whole work will not be finished for several years more. One aspect of Bruno's work which is relevant to my own is his assertion of the idea of intermedia (in the above-mentioned work): "True poetry is at the same time music and philosophy. True poetry and music are in a manner divine wisdom and painting." And so on, including painting (and, by implication, all visual art) in the mix.

Speculating on Bruno and poetry led me to start a new cycle of poems, the snowflake poems in what I call "snowflake form" because of their visual symmetry. Elements of these poems had been in my work for a long time, but the first full-fledged and conscious use of the visual cancrizan was in my poem "the snowflakes of giordano bruno," which I printed first as a Christmas card in 1978 and then, together with twenty-one other such snowflakes or sets of snowflakes, in the 1979 Printed Editions book *some recent snowflakes (and other things).* It also includes some translations by sound rather than sense, a kind of work which had preoccupied me for years, and which led me also to do another translation project in collaboration with Steve McCaffery and bp Nichol of Canada. In 1967 Robert Filliou had written a set of rock and roll lyrics which, however, proved too risqué for commercial broadcasting; so he published them with English translations by George Brecht and German ones by Diter Roth. In due course the book went out of print. We now (1978) published, with Membrane Press in Milwaukee, our "homophonic" translations, with myself translating Roth, Nichol (who speaks almost no French) doing Filliou's original French, and McCaffery doing a "homolinguistic" (his term) translation of Brecht's English into punned English. The result, *Six Fillious,* makes a handy paradigm of such things; but one book which is still needed, to establish the field, is an anthology of homophonic translations by many poets.

Way back in the start of my creative life I had thought of myself as primarily a musical composer, had studied with Henry Cowell and John Cage (among others), and music was still very much a part of my artistic consciousness. I continued to compose music through the 1960s and 1970s, and I strongly felt the need to create a body of music which would reflect the same concerns as I was working with in my writings and visual art. I therefore decided that the next focus for my publishing activity should be music. Naturally, I first submitted my music to conventional publishers, and after five or six rejections, it became clear that Printed Editions would have to undertake some music publishing. A suitable starting place seemed to be to do a collection of short piano pieces, which, in due course, materialized as *Piano Album: Short Piano Pieces, 1962–1984* (1980). The reason for the 1984 date in the title was that I wanted to make it clear that I was not going to compose some avalanche of piano pieces, opportunistically, for everyone who asked for one, that I would publish no additional short piano pieces until 1984 or later.

A short digression about printers seems necessary at this point. I had studied offset printing in the early 1960s, had worked in printing shops before I went into publishing, and, in the years when I was running the Something Else Press, I did most of the sophisticated camera work that was needed in our publications on a camera which was located wherever I lived at the time. I also designed a good many books for other publishers. Though I was not tempted to print our books myself—the ownership of this or that kind of press would have made me feel obliged to use this or that format for most of our books, as each press is most suitable for only a small number of possible formats. Even so, working closely with the printers that we used was the only way to achieve the results that were wanted, and we simply could not have afforded to buy some of the special effects I called for in my designs from outside sources. In the early 1970s I had settled "permanently" (as I hoped) in a small village in northern Vermont, which happened to be near the legendary Stinehour Press, the finest letterpress book printer in North America. Thus the presence of Stinehour Press is a factor in some of the editorial decisions of what book to do and what not to do. They printed *classic plays, Everyone Has Sher Favorite (His or Hers), George Herbert's Pattern Poems: In Their Tradition* and *some recent snowflakes (and other things).* Their offset division also printed *Piano Album.* But that book includes a couple of graphic notations which, like most of my graphics use the human nude. They had troubles with this. I was also then planning out *of celebration of morning,* which is in part a celebration of the body of its young protagonist, Justin. When they set the type for that book, there was no problem. But when they actually saw the mechanics for it with all the photographs, they decided not to do the book. So I realized it was time to find another printer—and therefore, presumably, another home for myself.

A poet friend of mine, George Quasha, had started a small printing firm in the mid-1970s called Open

Studio, which specialized in artists books and literature. As the public funding for such work dried up at the turn of the decade, while other printers went under or searched more desperately for grants, Quasha decided instead to move into the area of commercial viability, specifically into the field of high quality printing. He therefore seemed like an appropriate neighbor and so I bought a small church, parsonage, and parish house up the hill from his home and editorial and art facilities. That is where I and Printed Editions now reside, and, except for *celebration,* he has printed all the recent books, not just for myself but for the other Printed Editions authors as well.

If *foew&ombwhnw* is a sort of summing up of whatever I had achieved up to 1969, then *of celebration of morning* (1980), my most complex single work to date, sums up my experience of the 1970s. On the one hand it is a story: the homoerotic (if not necessarily homosexual) celebration by an older man (not necessarily myself) of a younger one, who dies at the end of an overdose of heroin. The story is told in a cycle of poems which moves through the year from August to July, most of them in my snowflake form and following the theory of narrative I have referred to before, as one finds it in the Schlegel brothers. It also uses the same cyclical temporal structure as *7.7.73* and celebrates nature (including the human figure) in the same way. It also uses a thematic set of photographs, almost all of Justin, some of which have poems, mostly in snowflake form, written after the photographs. Most photographic images are presented in several forms, as line drawings or as photoderivations, in one form or another. The styles of these visual materials are more appropriate to the narrator (unnamed) than to myself—which is to say that they are more like snapshots than like traditional art photographs; similarly, the line drawings are not of a fine art type but are more like comic book illustrations. The layout of the book is mostly off-square, askew, like a scrapbook rather than an art book. There are other strands to the braid too—a set of I Ching trigrams and hexagrams, providing a second cycle. Each page is called a "world"—"world 1," "world 2," and so on. A second, less systematic arrangement of the pages was determined by chance operations, giving an aleatoric factor: this sequence is given by the instruction on all pages (except page 60, where the printer left it off by mistake) to "Go to World 35," for example, and on "World 35" one is instructed to "Go to World 3." The poem on the month of May is nonexistent: its place is taken by a piece of music, "Long Arch," which is in snowflake form, a cancrizan. At every stage, all the elements interpenetrate—like a braid, as I said before. All in all, it is a "polysemiotic fiction" (my phrase on the title page) in which each element points to the others. There are also questions on every page, mostly chosen from remarks which the model said at one time or another, others which seemed suitable for the narrator, and few which deal with the fact that this is, in various ways, a book about a book—it is not "*a* celebration of morning" but "*of* celebration of morning"—or perhaps "of celebration of *mourning*," since there is little question but that this young man is in some way doomed, either to grow old (and to become himself like the narrator?) or, as it happens, to die. It is a complex book but, I hope, not indecipherable; I could not have achieved my desired result in a simpler way. The reader simply takes the work and makes what he will of it—a perfect work for my new audience-centered theoretical focus, of which more momentarily. It was also a suitable good-bye to my literary emphasis in the 1970s, since it was clear to me then that I must explore the implications of my work in music in a more rigorous way.

The reason for doing ambiguous work of this sort is to allow the participants—performers or readers or whatever—to use their own experience and capabilities in developing the eventual meaning of the work. This is nowhere more true than in my next Printed Editions book, *Ten Ways of Looking at a Bird* (1981), whose title is a playful variation on the name of a poem by Wallace Stevens whose work I have always admired, though, goodness knows, there is no modern poet more different from myself. This is a piece for violin and harpsichord; the harpsichord part is developed in "live time" (that is, during the performance) from what the violinist is doing, according to a set of rules. The violinist uses musical staves set over a set of ten blue photographs of the same model that I used in *celebration;* each movement uses a different gamut, or set of up to seven notes, which he may use in any octave or transposition, but which are the *only* notes he uses in any performance of that movement. Just *what* notes he uses is determined by his own skills and unique abilities—no "fully composed" realizations could take advantage of all the skills of all violinists—but there are also rules for using the photographs.

Twenty-Six Mountains for Viewing the Sunset From (1981) is for a small ensemble, including three dancers. It is a different kind of notation, not using photographs but using an indication of what kinds of textures and patterns are desired. The title comes from a trip I took late one night with a teenager from Vermont, who brought me to some of his favorite places to view the sunset from; it was magical evening, and I wanted to celebrate it in this twenty-six movement piece, each movement of which is characterized, somehow, by a fanciful description of a mountain which might or might not be spoken aloud at the time of the performance.

Sonata for Prepared Piano (1982) is a short work which, again, uses photoderivations as parts of the notation—this time nature with incomplete figure photographs, mostly obscured by the natural objects around them.

Variations on a Natural Theme (1982) is a large orchestral work, in some ways a companion to the *Ten Ways,* since this time it uses gamuts (in this case selected by the individual musicians) and photoderivations made from a female model; she was insistent that she not be recognizable, since she was a teacher and was afraid that it would be damaging to her professionally if it were known that she had posed for figure photographs. This was fine by me, since it fitted in with my plans to use very extreme derivations which are, at times, difficult to relate to the human figure at all. If performed, the work would sound rather like the *Ten Ways.* Socially the work interests me too, since it means that each musician must act creatively to work out his or her part and must therefore take the responsibility to make it sound according to his vision. Most musicians in most performances are near-automatons, and that does not accord with how I think human beings should be, especially in artistic situations—they should be (and the audience as well) as alert as the spectators at a boxing match, empathizing with each thrust and event, seeing where it all goes, and fitting into their own roles appropriately.

With *Variations* I have created musical paradigms to accord with my musical and visual art practice, and so my musical publishing can now become more intermittent. But what is next to do?

The theory that I set forth in *Dialectic of Centuries* lacked a teleology—I needed to state what the purpose of my practice (and the practice of many of my contemporaries) is and to suggest what was offered to the recipient of the work—performer, audience, reader, viewer, and so on. This lack was made up in an essay, "Horizons," which focuses on the fusion that occurs when the horizon of the recipient meets the horizon of the creator, myself or otherwise. I also needed a taxonomy of the works of my contemporaries, in the intermedia (visual poetry, sound poetry, etc.) and otherwise. This makes manifest the need for a second theory book, presumably to be called "Horizons," to develop these areas and to complete the critical system into which my work and that of so many contemporaries falls. Otherwise our learned brethren will come along and say, "This work does not do what X does (Beethoven, Pound, the structuralists, Picasso, whoever); therefore it is boring and not good." It is my task to point out not only wherein it is not boring but where the pleasure lies—an erotic of the new work is needed, and also, in such a taxonomy, to deal with the historical problems of such work, that they have a pedigree as old as that of mankind itself.

It would also be appropriate to prepare a collection of my early works, since few of these were collected into *foew&ombwhnw;* many of them were published in mimeographed booklets as acting scripts and suchlike. I should show the steps which led me to what I subsequently did, as parallel to the ratiocinations and inner arguments which philosophers use, to establish not only the validity of their points but as part of the points themselves; it is sometimes as important to show the paths one did not take as to show the course that one followed.

The collection of early visual poems and the homophonic anthology, both already mentioned, are well worth doing; I cannot afford to do them with Printed Editions, but perhaps some trade publisher would like to do them some day.

The Bruno translation should be completed, and "The Colors" should be published as what it is—the keystone cycle of my aleatoric texts. Perhaps my early novel, "Orpheus Snorts," should be published—it too relates to all this, since it follows a geometrical structure as well as its plot and is therefore in some sense an intermedial work.

What I do *not* want to do is to have a career, in the sense of filling commissions that do not tie in with my actual interests, to get my name into print "in all the right places" and anthologies; there are quite enough of those already (and of course these have their role, but not in the sense of keeping me from doing what only I can do—my real work). My real career should be, as I am currently fond of saying, a trajectory of satisfactions. And in that trajectory, each book should define a necessary and inevitable point in the trajectory as a whole, clearly related to the other points in the trajectory. Or perhaps, in my case, a better analogy would be to a "braid" of themes and interests, since I have chosen all the arts as my media or intermedia; each strand of the braid moves in a parallel direction to the others, intertwined with it and making up the characteristic quality of the whole. Make no mistake: no work was ever worth reading/watching/seeing/hearing *because* it was intermedial—many wonderful artists cannot, with integrity, move in more than one medium. My work is only intermedial because I am a child of my time, and because I am who I am—it is simply my nature to be that way.

Glossary

Some of the words in this book are unfamiliar or are used in a special sense; for this reason, the following glossary of terms may be useful.

aleatoric: constructed by chance techniques.

allusive referential: a displacement from what one might expect at a given moment in a work toward some anticipated direction. Example: the moon is green. Nobody has ever seen a green moon in nature, but the image may have poetic or emotional validity.

anarchy: a condition of existence governed by no rational order.

chance operations: the techniques of aleatoric constructions, for example, the use of the I ching, dice, or computerized random digits to "scramble," as it were, a list of items.

event: a minimal unit in an artwork or performance or music.

exemplativism: artworks which imply other, equally valid alternatives. Such a work is merely an example of a whole set, which it implies.

expression: either the usual meaning, of concretizing the emotional or intellectual state of someone by presenting it, or the designation of a symbolic mathematical form or an aesthetic one.

expressionism: the concept that art should express the artist, emotionally and intellectually. This concept characterized a historical movement in the fine arts in the early twentieth century, but in this book the term is seldom historical.

gamut: a set of notes or materials in a given work which are the only ones used in that work.

happening: an intermedial (q.v.) performance work which, by its nature, represents a conceptual fusion of visual art, literature, and music.

hermeneutics: the methodology of interpretation, in the tradition of Martin Heidegger and Hans-Georg Gadamer. Hermeneutic criticism tends to focus on the viewer or listener, to concern itself with how perception colors the work.

horizon: the metaphor of an ordinary horizon—the range of information, feelings, experiences, and imaginings associated with a given area on the part of an artist or of a viewer, reader, listner, etc.

Horizontverschmelzung: the fusion of horizons (q.v.). This is an essential term in Gadamer's hermeneutics (q.v.).

intention: a statement of the kind of elements which will compose a piece rather than the specific contents of that piece.

intermedia: when two or more discrete media are conceptually fused, they become intermedia. They differ from mixed media (q.v.) in being inseparable in the essence of an artwork.

Klangfarbenmelodie: melody of timbre rather than melody of pitch. This term is associated with the music of Arnold Schoenberg.

metataxis: a term in anthropology, covering the shift in function or social meaning of a thing or act; e.g., a bow-and-arrow, once a means of war or getting food, is now a sport or a toy.

mimetic: the adjectival form of *mimesis,* imitation. In art this means the representation of nature in a factual, literal sense.

mixed media: the presence in a work of two or more discrete media without their being conceptually fused. An example is the opera, in which there are music, visual art, and a literary text, but one always knows which is which. In this way the mixed media differ from intermedia (q.v.) and intermedial forms such as the happening.

modular music: a style of music in which melodic modules, or minimal groups of notes, are repeated over and over again, usually with slight variation, moving in and out of synchronization. This style developed in the 1960s and is associated with Steve Reich, Terry Riley, and Philip Glass, among others.

module: a uniform structural component, intended to be repeated often with some systematic modification.

objective: a theory of art, especially of literature, in which the work is intended as an object rather than as a process, for contemplation or consideration rather than as a source of energy itself. The concept is associated with T. S. Eliot and Ezra Pound, among others.

ostinato: in music, a module (q.v.) which is *not* varied.

poetry: either word-based art with musical or visual elements or both, using cognitive structures which convey content or musical or visual means as a substitute or augmentation of these; also, the quality of works traditionally associated with such art.

polyartisis: artists who work in more than one medium. The word was coined by Richard Kostelanetz ca. 1967.

postcognitive: the quality of works in which the self of the artist is not conveyed and no alternate persona is generated either. Such a self or persona is characteristic of Western art up to roughly the late 1950s, and the term

"postcognitive" is intended to characterize a large portion of the arts produced since that time.

pragmatic: in art, art which instructs, usually on a moral or social plain.

semiotics: the study of the conveyors of meaning.

sher: his-or-her.

sound poetry: poetry in which the emphasis is overwhelmingly on sound rather than on cognitive language or visual structures. Sound poetry is sometimes not written out but recorded directly on magnetic tape and other media.

taxonomy: the study of classifications and of the identifying aspects and structures of things, art styles, works, etc.

text-sound poetry: usually a synonym for "sound poetry" (q.v.), but more accurately for sound poetry which is written out in the form of a text. The term was coined by Richard Kostelanetz.

torque: the quality of a line in visual art, or a sound in a musical composition, etc., to convey energy. The term was a commonplace in the criticism associated with abstract expressionism, the main movement in American abstract art in the 1950s.

tutti: in a performance, the point at which all the performers play or perform together. Usually the term is used in music.

visual poetry: poetry in which the visual element predominates. The best-known genre of visual poetry is concrete poetry, modern poems using the letters of the alphabet in a visual way. But it also includes many other genres, such as poems using photographs or semiotic signs.

Index